FINDING MY GOOD THING

How God can lead you to your future spouse by dating with a spiritual purpose

BRYAN C. JONES

Dedication

This book is dedicated to the God of grace, mercy and love, the Creator of the Universe, Who created my Good Thing, my wife, Danielle. I dedicate this book to the God, Who had a plan for my life, the God Who was patient with me when my behavior didn't warrant any blessings. Thank you Lord! You are such an amazing God, Who has been so loving, kind, longsuffering and forgiving towards me. When I prayed to You asking You for someone I could love, someone who had a heart for You and someone who would stand beside me in support of the work You gave me to do, You did it! You are my Light, my Shield, my Fortress, my Protector and my Deliverer.

Father, I dedicate this book in reverence to You for providing my first example of a Godly obedient woman of God, my mother, Jo Ann. Lord, you have helped me learn so much through her willingness to serve, her obedience, bible study, commitment and her faith in trials and tribulations. Thank you Lord. Heavenly Father, my prayer is that You bless every single person who reads this book to put You first in their lives, allowing You to lead them to a spiritual, practicing child of God, as You did with me, so that this world will see Godly marriages modeled. God continue to give Danielle and me good works to do and sustain our ministry so that we can help You save, restore, and retain souls. Thank you, my Heavenly Father. You are an Awesome God!

TABLE OF CONTENTS

Seasons of Relationship Grace

Seasons of Relationship Growth

Seasons of Relationship Grace

INTRODUCTION

Imagine staring into the eyes of another human being so wonderfully and beautifully made by the Creator who belongs only to you. Realistically, it's certainly possible for you to find and operate in such a relationship with God remotely controlling the minds of two God fearing individuals whose lives are in submission to the Holy Spirit, who is constantly distributing love through the covenant commitment of the marriage bond. How awesome would it be if God blessed you not only with the person of your dreams, but with the person whom He created specifically just for you? The reality is the person who God ultimately and divinely has for your life to coexist with in a spiritual, loving, covenant bond called marriage is out there in this world.

Any person desirous of finding that special creation of God must simply begin the process of positioning himself/herself to allow God, and only God, to orchestrate such a relationship of love and bring it to fruition. This book *"Finding My Good Thing"* teaches readers the value of how getting into the purpose of God can position you to be poised and prepared for that special person the Creator had in mind for you even before you both were conceived.

How grateful would you be to the God, Who would create someone specifically just for you, if you trusted Him to bring that person into your life? Wait! All it takes for God to bless you is for you to take the leap of faith to begin your journey with God, working in His kingdom for His glory, allowing Him to divinely direct your path to the person whom He desires for you. The Lord did it for me, and this book is about how God can do it for you! To God be the glory!

Changing Your Who, What, When, and Why in Dating

Changing your reason for dating changes the way you view dating. Dating can be an exhausting and seemingly never-ending process if its participants have no purposeful goal to accomplish from the social experience we call dating. I always wanted a wife, but I used to date people for all the wrong reasons. I was trying to have fun, fishing in all the wrong places, sometimes using all the wrong bait and attracting all the wrong people, until I changed my reason for dating to a purposeful one that placed God first, and He eventually led me to the love of my life. For that reason, I wanted to share how the process of dating with a spiritual reason changed the way I began to view dating from a formerly shallow worldly experience to a beautiful purposeful experience.

Dating with a spiritual purpose is the process of being someone who desires to live a life according to God's will, being someone who wants to go to that place the Word of God refers to as heaven and living a life operating in the purpose of God, believing God will lead you to someone who wants to do the same. My heart simply breaks every time I see wonderful, intelligent, loving, spiritually gifted and talented men and women struggle in senseless relationships where the Lord has not been placed at the center of the relationship.

Changing your reason for dating changes the way you view dating.

In an effort to glorify God, I decided to write this book hoping that someone would learn from some of the many mistakes I've made and have often seen happen in the dating process. I strongly believe someone will also see what God blessed me to understand through my

2

positive and what I thought were negative experiences in dating. The process of dating with a spiritual purpose was a blessing for me, a person who has made a plethora of mistakes in the dating process, which makes me know that finding your "dream spouse" is attainable and possible for you through the spiritual process of dating with a purpose in mind. God is the reason I am writing this book, because it was He who led me to share my story and help singles, all over the world, who are looking to find their own good thing.

Who is This Book for?

This book is for Christians, Non-Christians, hopeless romantics, teenagers, young adults, the middle aged, seniors, divorcees, widows, virgins, non-virgins, and any unmarried person who desires to be married. *"Finding My Good Thing"* is also for married people who could find many helpful practical solutions, strategies, and glaring realities to help with their own marriage dynamic. This book can even be useful for people who are reading it to share this powerful information with children, church groups, social groups, book clubs, and as a great gift to any single person who aspires to get married. This book is for that person who can't seem to find anyone, the person who crosses every T and dots every I, but still has not found anyone. *"Finding My Good Thing"* is for the faithful child of God who works hard to live right, but frequently has what I call "Cold Fridays" and "Lonely Saturdays" and a voice in your head that says you're never going to find anyone.

This book is for those young, middle-aged, or older Preachers who are single, studying daily, preaching and watching God bless those you preach God's Word to who are finding people to spend their lives with, while you go home lonely after Church; this book is for you. This is for that person who has had so many so called "failed relationships" who now, as a result, has more baggage than every terminal at Hartsfield Jackson Airport in Atlanta, GA; this book is for you. In our current cultural climate, healthy spiritual behaviors in dating relationships aren't viewed as serious protocols that must be followed. Even in some Christian social circles, God is sometimes viewed as just a God that we vocally say we believe in, but unfortunately, in some dating relationships, God has never become the reason or genesis for determining our potential marriage relationship decisions.

This book is designed to encourage those who date to do so with a spiritual purpose, eliminating the practices of dating that have been detrimental to happiness and holiness, and to find a potential heaven-seeking mate for marriage, and become a power couple in the Kingdom whose goal is simply to please God.

I hope to empower someone to work for the Lord while being a single person as well as motivate every single reader to use their time as a single person as a weapon in God's kingdom. Of course, this book is packed with many dating tips, help with intimacy issues, do's and don'ts, and real heart wrenching testimonies of what God has done by blessing me with my dream spouse. If God did this for me, I know He can do it for you. In just ten months God did for me what I had failed to do for myself in twenty years of dating, gracefully blessing me with the love of my life, His choice for me to work for His kingdom, My Good Thing!

The Five Types of Singles

What kind of single person are you? There are typically **five types of single persons** that we can identify. There are those who are *Single and Searching*, *Single and Satisfied*, *Single and Salty*, *Single and Slipping* **and** *Single and Settled.*

Single and Searching

"Ask, and it will be given to you; seek, and you will find; knock, and it will be opened to you. "For everyone who asks receives, and he who seeks finds, and to him who knocks it will be opened." **Matthew 7:7-8**

The single and searching person is one who actively seeks and pursues potential friendships with the opposite sex in hopes that one of those friendships may flourish into a future dating relationship. As searchers, these singles seek to meet people through various avenues where they can interact with potential dating candidates at events, functions, dating websites, socials, church or the "hook up" through a mutual friend. Many of these singles have active personal social media profiles on dating websites in efforts to be linked with a compatible mate for marriage. Some of the popular dating websites have advertising commercials which boast success stories of encounters where people have found their mates for marriage online. However, these websites and commercials do not tell you the occurrences of horror stories, manipulation and scams many people have experienced from online dating. Persons who use the online method of interaction should be mindful of the pro's and con's of searching through various social media platforms.

Active singles who are searching in my estimation constantly have thoughts of potentially meeting that special someone and to that end, will make the efforts to initiate the initial contact when given the opportunity. There is nothing wrong being the catalyst who initiates the conversation, just make sure that you have a standard and criteria you're committed to that is conducive to obtaining healthy relationships. Remember, it's all about God's timing as it pertains to relationships, not your timing.

Single and Satisfied

> *"Not that I speak from want, for I have learned to be content in whatever circumstances I am."* **Philippians 4:11**

These singles have experienced some good and bad dating relationships or maybe even a marriage in the past, but they are not actively seeking dating candidates for marriage. These singles are content with where they currently are, but optimistic that a future dating relationship will materialize at some point. They are happy with who they are as a single person and being a child of God. The satisfied single is usually happy with their career, family and life in general even if they never get married. Those who are single and satisfied will go to movies by themselves, enjoy retail therapy, usually have good credit, will go to Starbucks alone to read a book and love spending time with friends and family. These singles enjoy their independence and typically don't consider their state as a single person miserable as some conclude, but one of freedom and self-sufficiency. These singles love the Lord and believe their time will eventually come if God has marriage in His plan for their lives. Those who are single and satisfied are focused on accomplishing their goals and preparing themselves for that person that God may have for them, if it's His will.

Single and Salty

These singles are what I call and coin as "salty", meaning they have been hurt significantly by people in past relationships and that hurt has manifested itself in their perspective of relationships and their attitude towards future relationships as a negative one. The salty singles have gotten to the point where they view dating, relationships and marriage in a negative light which has been influenced by their own negative experiences in relationships. Some salty singles have experienced a negative side of relationships that will forever impact their thinking which is an unfortunate reality. They have been cheated on, lied on, lied to, mistreated, misled, misused and made to feel inferior. Many have suffered traumatic emotional, physical and social abuse for years. Some of the saltiness these singles feel derives from experiencing the betrayal of people whom they loved, but that love wasn't reciprocated in past relationships, making their view of future relationships an opportunity to potentially experience more hurt. Although some of these singles are adamantly against ever being in another serious relationship or marriage, it is always helpful for them to learn how those negative relationships materialized. What mindset, decisions and people directly factored into the existence of those kinds of hurtful relationships in the past? If you have been salty towards seeing a glimmer of positive light in relationships because of your past, see the chapter in the book, called "The Blessing in the Breakup".

Single and Slipping

"Now the deeds of the flesh are evident, which are: immorality, impurity, sensuality, idolatry, sorcery, enmities, strife, jealousy, outbursts of anger, disputes, dissensions, factions, envying, drunkenness, carousing, and things like these, of which I forewarn you, just as I have forewarned you, that those who practice such things will not inherit the kingdom of God." **Galatians 5:19**

This particular kind of single person usually appears to be a wild child behaviorally. Slipping is an indication that they have slipped into the practice of sin, moral lapses and failures. These singles exhibit behaviors such as sleeping around, joyously experimenting in whatever and with whoever they can. These singles may be untrustworthy, party types, possibly charming, even attractive, but they demonstrate suspicious behavior. Some singles who are slipping have abandoned their moral and ethical beliefs as a result of being hurt, heartbroken and harmed because of how their last few relationships ended. They feel that slipping is a way to redeem their confidence or give pay back to their "ex" by going out to see who they can attract, believing that behavior will liberate or justify them to feel good about themselves again. But in reality, that slippage is an unhealthy coping mechanism to mask the pain of past rejection and betrayal. The excessive partying and drinking that leads to making bad decisions could be potential warning signs that this single person has slipped into sinful behavior that isn't conducive to being attractive for someone who's looking for a serious dating prospect.

For this single, one must consider if the behavior is a random occurrence, but isn't who this person really is or is the behavior consistent with a person's need to be involved both socially and sexually with multiple partners as a consistent lifestyle. No matter how attractive they are or how much money they have, be aware of the signs of a person that is consistently single and slipping.

Single and Settled

Typically, this single person is your middle aged or aged person who has maybe been through a marriage or two and possibly been through the unpleasant misfortune of having a deceased spouse. Some of these settled singles take the position that they WILL NEVER get married again under any condition. They wouldn't mind having a friend for social interaction, but are adamantly against the commitment of a marriage, being a person who has found value in individuality. This person could even be younger with or without children or older with grown children and is settled where they are in life. It's possible that the settled single is simply settled in their ways, being used to living by themselves, unwilling to alter their personal preferences for the sake of a committed marriage. The settled singles yearn to have their own personal independence and aren't willing to significantly compromise on anything at this particular stage of their lives. Some settled singles may be divorced and widowed seniors who have lived single for years and believe the only relationship they need is a relationship with Jesus Christ, which is the only marriage they want to have for the rest of their lives. This single and settled position is perfectly okay for the single person who decides to choose this route.

Some settled singles are much younger and have experienced the heartbreak of coming from broken families and households and they have made up their mind that marriage isn't for them based on the experiences which influenced their perception of marriage.

Lastly, some are single and settled because of financial reasons that may involve business ventures, inheritances, properties, assets or trust accounts that will be past down to them. These settled singles are not interested in marrying as it could interfere with their wealth. They refuse to engage in a marriage relationship that could potentially end in divorce for fear of losing a portion of their assets, so they prefer to be settled and unmarried which protects their financial assets. They may seek social companionship and even a sexual relationship, but these singles will tell you, "marriage isn't for me".

CHAPTER 1

Finding My Good Thing

"*Finding My Good Thing*" is all about how **God can lead you to marriage through purpose driven dating.** When purpose is present in a dating dynamic it should always be preceded by dedication, desire, and determination. Christians must have a desire, determination, and a dedicated lifestyle which propels, prompts, and prepares them to make spiritual decisions especially when it comes to dating. Dating with a spiritual purpose involves purposefully making a decision to marry someone who loves God more than they love you, desiring to live a life according to God's will and deciding to marry someone who wants to go to heaven just as badly as you do. In Proverbs 18:22 the writer says, *"He who finds a wife finds a good thing and obtains favor from the LORD."* **There's a difference between finding a wife and marrying a woman.** Not every woman is a wife, which means every woman desirous of marriage may not be your good thing. *God only releases His favor when finders find a wife, who God declares is a good thing!* (Proverbs 18:22)

God can lead you to marriage through purpose driven dating.

At some point in the past many of you may admit as I can that we took the Frank Sinatra approach to dating as the words in one of his songs said, "I did it my way." Unfortunately, dating my way in the past landed me into chaos, confusion, and frustration, so the first half of *"Finding My Good Thing"* introduces readers to what I call the **Seasons of Relationship Grace** where the reader discovers the pitfalls and dangers of dating with the wrong purpose desiring our way of doing things which usually culminates in unhealthy dating relationships that are devoid of spiritual substance but potent with pain. But thank God for His grace and mercy which gives those who love Him an opportunity to learn from those past mistakes by putting together the pieces of the relationship puzzle, doing things His way, for His glory.

The second half of *"Finding My Good Thing"* addresses solutions and practical behaviors which a believer who has a relationship with Jesus Christ can follow as they strive to accomplish their goal of marriage God's way. I call this part **Seasons of Relationship Growth,** where singles start to realize the big picture of purpose driven dating and working for the Lord; it gives an honest soul who desires a mate for marriage the absolute best chance for God to unfold a person who could operate in His purpose with you in a co-existing love affair with Him. Men and women of faith must never settle, expect mediocrity, or operate with a mundane mindset, but faithfully trust that God has already worked things out when mankind is trying to figure things out in your life. Following God's instructions and choosing to date someone who provides consistent, complimentary, spiritual behaviors can usher you into a fruitful marriage with someone God had in mind for you when you decide to let Him dictate what and who is right for you in a marriage through the dating process.

CHAPTER 2

Purpose Driven Dating

Dating can be an awesome experience or a terrible one, but for the child of God it MUST always have a purpose. If you want to ultimately be married, then you have to date with that purpose in mind. Let's be real, that's not how most people date these days. Frequently, I talk to people who are dating and they seem so happy and the relationship looks like it's headed toward marriage and sometimes I say, *"Have you set a wedding date yet?"* or *"When is the big day?"* Then the answer is usually *"I don't know."* *"Well, how long have you been dating?"* The answers I receive to that question are sometimes *five years, ten years* or the worst: *we've been together for so long I can't even remember."* Marriage has to be the goal, the desire, and the end game for the spiritually minded person that uses dating as a tool to determine potential, spiritual likeminded candidates for marriage.

Dating is certainly an interesting concept which carries a variety of definitions depending on which person you ask, as dating usually means different things to different people. I've seen too many people experience terrible emotional pain when they discover that

Have you set a wedding date yet?"

13

their definition of dating differs from the person they are dating because they assume dating means the same thing for each party associated, but nine times out of ten it doesn't. Some people view dating as a means to simply enjoy having a companion, but never intend to ever develop a long term serious relationship that leads to marriage with the person they are dating. Others view dating as a means to determine whether a person is deep enough into the dating relationship so that they can comfortably engage in a sexual relationship with someone. Subsequently, it's unfortunate that many men and women allow the emotional connection and physical attraction of the person they are dating to become the determining factor, which sometimes causes them to make a bad decision to sleep with someone they really don't know, in many cases, and have literally no true feelings for them. The enemy has deceived many men and women in our secular societies to accept being involved in sexual relationships before marriage. This acceptance of sexual promiscuity and sin has been perpetuated into the psyche of many people by those with social influence who teach that sexual immorality can be permitted after a certain period in the dating relationship as mentioned in our secular movies and music, which condone and promote premarital sexual activity in a dating relationship, which is addressed in the section titled, *CELEBRATING CELIBACY.*

In this book, we will define dating as a process that determines whether a person of the opposite sex should be considered as a candidate for marriage. Simply put, the word DATING directly involves the root word date, which is something people

> *In this book, we will define dating as a process that determines whether a person of the opposite sex should be considered as a candidate for marriage.*

who desire to get married should aspire to obtain a DATE, TIME, PLACE, and PERSON to become married to. Without ascertaining a specific date, you will not have a time, place, period, or person where you can comfortably say on this date, I am getting married to the person God has for my life. So as you date you are determining who you are going to set a date with to see whether this person has what you need in a spiritual spouse, if not it would be wise to give that dating relationship an expiration date.

Trust God and be Yourself When Dating

Beliefs, borders, and boundaries must be set early in the dating friendship if you have someone you are interested in, because they need to know what your definition of dating is; and you must ascertain their definition of dating for yourself as well. Dating is necessary to really get to know a person. Men and women have complimentary characteristics, physical, intellectual, and social characteristics that naturally attract them to one another. However, you probably should desire someone who is genuine that can complement you, not someone who is catering to you only for the sake of obtaining you without you knowing much about them.

In the movie Coming to America, Eddie Murphy's character was Akeem who was an African Prince of a wealthy Country called Zamunda. Murphy's character was involved in an arranged marriage set up by his parents. The woman who Murphy's father arranged for him to marry was played by Vanessa Bell Calloway, whose character didn't have a personality, mind or an opinion of her own. In his feeble attempt to communicate with her, every question Akeem (Murphy) asked her to get to know her she boldly responded with "Whatever you like…""Whatever

15

you like…" Though some may find this kind of non-existing personality appealing, that type of behavior simply does not involve the gender complimentary characteristics that God has given males and females, nor does having a servant actually compliment or help with the need for social and intellectual attractiveness or engagement for men and women. It's a powerful experience when you find someone who has integrity and consistently remain who they are, without compromising their spiritual integrity, while bringing something admirable to the table themselves.

I was blessed by God to have those gender complimentary characteristics deeply embedded into my wife, Danielle, in which I found most appealing. I can vividly remember meeting Danielle for our first date at Zaxby's, a fast food restaurant in the South. I know what you're thinking, how cheap of you Preacher! You asked her out to Zaxby's for your first date? Well, yes, but it's complicated. Technically, I had a strategy; the place we planned to meet wasn't my focus. My focus was to get to know her, so I didn't really care where we met, nor did she, as we were both excited to get together for the first time. After preaching in Anderson, SC, I contacted her to have some coffee in her hometown, but I didn't know the area of Seneca, SC well, so I asked her where we could go to talk for a few minutes and we decided that from the direction I was coming from, Zaxby's was the closest restaurant. My plan was to simply have a conversation with her and that is what we did. I made it clear that I had seen her many times and I was shocked that she was single.

From there, three hours went by like it was three minutes! I couldn't tell you anything about anyone else who was in the restaurant or what was going on around us, all I know is that I was engaged in a *get to know you*" conversation with an intellectually, mature, beautiful woman of God. It was the conversation I'd dreamed of having my whole life. I do remember buying a drink and keeping that Styrofoam Zaxby's cup for a long time. Yes, I kept a used Zaxby's drink cup in my car as a memento because that cup reminded me of the conversation I had with my future wife. After three hours, it was time for me to travel back to Atlanta, GA where I lived at the time, as I commuted back and forth to Anderson, SC to preach. We hugged each other and all I can remember thinking was how hard it was to leave her. After one conversation, it felt like I'd known her my whole life. My point for telling you this is that when you date a person there's no need to be distracted by all the things people do in dating which negatively impact a true, genuine, and real conversation. It's okay to ask questions as straight-up friends to truly get to know someone in whom you're interested.

I remember many years before I met my wife, there was a time in my life when I thought dating was about wining and dining, consequently devaluing the importance of communication. On one occasion I remember dating a young lady who I frequently took out to dinner, we went to movies and always used some form of entertainment as the center of our focus and attention. I always paid for everything, which wasn't a problem, but after many expensive meals and entertainment expenses I assumed that at some point since we were just friends and seeing that-she asked me to go out to places, she would at least offer to pay for parking, offer a tip or something, but she never would, and it began to frustrate me sometimes. I knew she had a job somewhere, but sadly, I never knew if she even had a bank account, a debit or credit card or any cash because she never offered to pay for anything. After about six months we finally had a real conversation that was more than just a mere surface conversation and it was without the accompaniment of any entertainment, then I realized I wasn't interested in her at all. We really shared no commonalities; we weren't on the same page spiritually and had differing views on almost everything. I thought to myself, "if I had only had this conversation six months ago, I could have saved time, money, energy, effort, and been much closer to meeting someone I actually liked."

The point is when you are dating you need to ASK the tough important *GET TO KNOW YOU* questions upfront or you can waste time you don't have. Ask some open ended spiritual questions like these: *Tell me about your parents? What kind of relationship do you have with your parents? Are you close with your family or relatives? What is your ideal family dynamic? How important is having children to you? Define being happy? Give me an example of what you did on a day that you enjoyed? What is your most successful accomplishment? Tell me something interesting about your thoughts of me? Tell me something about you that most people don't know? Who is the most important person in your life? How do you define dating? How do you define friendship between the opposite sex? What was the last good sermon you heard about and what did you do as a result of hearing it? How adventurous are you, give me an example? Is physical attraction important to you? If so, how much does physical and spiritual attraction weigh in your decision making in choosing to be with someone? What motivates you? Do you have any children? How will you raise your children? What governs your life? What is your specific purpose for dating and what do you hope to accomplish in dating relationships? Is getting married one day one of your goals? Do you know Jesus? Describe your relationship with Jesus and what does Jesus means to you? What is marital commitment to you? What's your favorite passage of scripture and why is it your favorite? What is your commitment to*

ASK the tough important

GET TO KNOW YOU

questions upfront

attending church? Some may say that sounds like an interview. Yes! They are interviewing for the job of becoming your spouse and one flesh with you and God, which is a pretty big deal and calls for some in-depth questions. These are just some questions which could and should be addressed in conversation early into any friendship.

CHAPTER 3

Dating Under the Influence

D ating, like any other thing, can be negatively or positively influenced by people, problems, places, or predicaments. One should ask the question as to what has influenced my thinking as I go in and out of dating relationships. What and who has shaped your thinking in regard to your relationship views? What has shaped your idea of healthy dating relationships? How did you learn and what relationship behaviors should be tolerated or accepted? Where did you get your overall approach toward relationships and dating? Somehow, something or someone influenced your thinking toward relationships in your past and the likelihood is high that particular influence became the foundation of how you began to formulate what's acceptable or unacceptable behavior in a relationship.

What has shaped your idea of healthy dating relationships?

If you knew someone who used foul language, sex, drugs, alcohol, and pills, who displayed behavior under the influence of those substances in a relationship, the chances are it affected your thinking. I'll never forget an example of tolerating and accepting unhealthy relationship behavior that I witnessed in high school by a teenage boy and girl. The girl was talking to another boy, a friend presumably, and her boyfriend saw it as he walked up to her locker and got in her face and berated her saying, "Why were you talking to him?" "What did I tell you about that?" He had her cornered in front of an open locker as if he was about to beat her and she immediately became docile and submitted to his influence believing her behavior was wrong. Before this, I had never seen seriousness like this in a high school dating relationship. Witnessing this myself was incredible and fascinating, and it wasn't the only experience I saw in school where behavior like this was normal.

Where did this guy get this type of abusively threatening, controlling behavior? How was he so easily able to convince her she was disrespecting him and that what she was doing was wrong? How did he learn to physically intimidate the young girl as if he was going to physically abuse her? Where did the young girl learn to accept this kind of verbal and physically threatening treatment which caused her to submit to repenting because of her actions for fear of losing this kind of relationship in high school? In this scenario the behavior displayed by both teenagers all stemmed from influences. I was negatively impacted by that interaction because that behavior is what I saw some of my peers do in relationships. Fortunately, my behavior was never affected by what I saw, but I never forgot it, and it still influenced me just by seeing it.

If a young boy has a high level of respect for his father, he follows him around, emulates him and idolizes him; but if he consistently sees his father struggle watching his mother commit infidelity, leaving his father time after time, that behavior will undoubtedly influence the boy. As a result of what he saw, the young boy's thinking was negatively shaped in regard to relationships. Consequently, witnessing that type of unacceptable behavior could adversely cause the young man to decide that since his father didn't deserve that treatment, the young boy vows never to allow that kind of scenario to take place in any of his own future relationships.

Potentially, the child's accepted views towards his own future relationships were tainted, ruined before he ever even got into a serious relationship because of the negative influences he observed in his family dynamic. This young boy could grow up to be the brother that stalks women, doesn't trust them to tell the truth, frequently calling or texting trying to ascertain whereabouts, or he could even become physically, emotionally, and even spiritually abusive because of his influences, experiences, and his decision not to tolerate certain behavior to avoid the hurt his father experienced.

Likewise, if a young daughter watches her father run around and display unfaithfulness it could lead her as a woman to become scared, having witnessed her mother become negatively impacted by her father's actions, causing many insecurities because of unhealthy relationship influences.

It all starts with people being under the influence of relationships that create a pattern of acceptable or unacceptable behavior in their thinking. Personal insecurities can also destroy relationships, but something causes the thinking that exposes our minds to be influenced by the fears that insecurities birth, which could result in experiencing lots of pain in relationships. In contrast, if a woman has been exposed to seeing someone she respects go through an abusive relationship, it could influence her to do the same. If a man or woman has insecurities about their appearance or low self-esteem within themselves, that kind of insecurity could negatively impact their thinking causing them to believe that they don't deserve to be treated like a King or Queen or to believe they can't do any better, thus, mentally conforming to the negative influences.

Unfortunately, many times people never get over the things they have heard said about them or someone they loved, permanently affecting their thinking about relationships. As a result of our influences, many people commit relationship sabotage and never have a clue as to the fact that certain experiences, factors, and forces having been engrained into their thinking toward accepted behaviors in dating. That's why it's so paramount to date with a spiritual purpose so that you have a better chance to operate, maintain, and be joined together with someone who is under the influence of the Holy Spirit, giving you a better chance to have a healthy spiritual relationship.

Relationships are joint unions with God which must be worked on consistently to become as healthy and as holy as possible. God desires healthy Christian relationships which is what every person aspiring to become married must strive for and that starts in the dating phase.

Being exposed to the wrong influences is certainly not a relationship death sentence. You can rise up to higher spiritual heights to eliminate the kind of behaviors that being exposed to the wrong influences may have caused. The beauty of a relationship with the Lord is that it can aid, assist, and attract you to the spiritual and biblical influences that promote healthy relationship behaviors, which can lead to a Godly marriage. No matter how bad or toxic your thinking or behavior has been, God has the power to show you another way, a better way to find someone He has in mind for you; so never give up on finding love.

Love is worth spending a lifetime finding. *"If I speak with the tongues of men and of angels, but do not have love, I have become a noisy gong or a clanging cymbal. If I have the {gift of prophecy}, and know all mysteries and all knowledge; and if I have all faith, so as to remove mountains, but do not have love, I am nothing. And if I give all my possessions to feed {the poor}, and if I surrender my body to be burned, but do not have love, it profits me nothing. Love is patient, love is kind {and} is not jealous; love does not brag {and} is not arrogant, does not act unbecomingly; it does not seek its own, is not provoked, does not take into account a wrong {suffered}, does not rejoice in unrighteousness, but rejoices with the truth; bears all things, believes all things, hopes all things, endures all things. Love never fails;..." (1 Corinthians 13:1-8)*

The Satire of Relationship Sabotage

Many relationships are over before they even begin because those involved are not healed from the previous relationship, but bounce back into a new relationship with the same baggage that systematically destroyed their last relationship. Since everyone carries some level of baggage into their relationships, I'm writing this section to empower someone to improve their quality of life by embracing, establishing, and educating oneself of the new identity God provides for His people who have a relationship with Jesus Christ, despite the emotional rollercoaster of some negative life experiences. Before one can really have a healthy relationship with anyone there needs to be an attempt to uncover the root of the issues that plagued our behavior in past relationships. Otherwise, you will enter into many relationships, but come out of every one of them being the same person, never realizing that you could be sabotaging every relationship. Most of us have been emotionally hurt, bruised and battered, and that hurt manifests itself in our behaviors, personalities, and willingness to trust and in our self confidence. Unless you are willing to grab a shovel and dig deep into your life for clues as to what it was that caused your accepted behavior, things could get worse.

In order to gain a steady dose of acceptable healthy relationship behavior, a person has to work each day to **deprogram** their mind from all the past influences which may have negatively impacted their thinking towards relationships and **reprogram** their minds daily, depositing positive influences from spiritually driven relationships which will positively affect their thinking. If people have never been exposed to a positive spiritual relationship then they just don't know how good a relationship can be when God is really the Center of it. What influences have you been dating under? Were some negative and some positive? Dating under the wrong influences can cause physical pain, emotional strain, limited spiritual motivation and could even cause death as a result of tolerating a toxic abusive relationship dynamic.

Catfish are bottom dwellers or bottom feeders who instinctively and consistently seek to be fed from the bottom of the water. Unlike catfish, salmon instinctively know when it's time to swim upstream because they have a purpose to spawn, depositing eggs in the place where they were originally born. When salmon swim upstream they have to fight against the currents of the oceans, lakes, and rivers, but they aren't deterred because they have a purpose to deposit eggs for breeding. As believers, the catfish mentality will make it difficult to walk in God's purpose if you are constantly allowing yourself to be fed negativity by negative people, dwelling in negative places. Who is hindering you from having a progressive spiritual dating relationship? Who is constantly feeding you negativity? What crowd of people surrounding you makes it difficult for you to operate in your purpose of dating the right person? What negative thought or mindset have you allowed to keep you stuck on the bottom of the relationship chain? Make the decision to have the salmon mentality and swim upstream, fighting through the challenges of life, learning from the past, seeking to fulfill your purpose of making spiritual deposits into the lives of mankind. The Word of God teaches us that bad company, corrupts good morals (1 Cor 15:33). You may have or had good morals, but the bad company you allow to feed you can corrupt the good morals that exist within you. Make God's purpose, your purpose by aligning yourself with people and goals that align with your spiritual purpose and decide to swim upstream as you fight against the forces which desire to hinder you. Give God all the glory!

So, it's the relationship with Christ that can sever the influences that hinder healthy relationships and break the chains, strains, and strongholds of behaviors detrimental to the divine destiny our Deliverer desires for dedicated Disciples. You can positively change your influences once you graduate from your seasons of grace to your seasons of growth.

STUDY GUIDE

1) Acknowledge within yourself the relationship influences which have influenced the way you operate in dating relationships or a past marriage.

2) Accept the fact that dysfunctional thinking may have existed in your behaviors in past relationships on your part, if you displayed dating behavior that may have affected the outcome of some of your relationships.

3) Write down three dating behaviors that were a result of positive spiritual influences that were good. Also, write down three dating behaviors that were a result of negative influences that opposed God's will. Discuss these influences either positive or negative with a close confidant or in a small group setting. Share at least one positive or negative spiritual relationship characteristic that you plan to work on individually each day so that you will be better prepared the next time God allows you to meet someone who may be a potential candidate for marriage.

CHAPTER 4

The Danger of Being Too Thirsty

Are you thirsty, really thirsty, dangerously thirsty for a relationship? How thirsty are you to be involved with someone and to what extent would you compromise the things you really want, just to be involved into the dating relationship that has been and will always be headed nowhere? Check your relationship thirst level as it could lead to the volatility of having bad relationships, being blinded by obvious signs and the red flags that should have forced you to end those kinds of relationships. Many times both men and women are willing to compromise their family values, standards, beliefs, personal safety and even their moral integrity to be with someone that they truthfully don't even like. Some fear being alone and would rather be with someone instead of being with no one and unfortunately make unwise, unspiritual decisions to be with someone who isn't complimentary to what they bring to the table.

When Lust Disguises Itself As Love

One of the worst things you can do in a dating relationship is compromise your spiritual integrity. Consequently, as

One of the worst things you can do in a dating relationship is compromise your spiritual integrity.

a direct result of this kind of travesty, some people end up placing their spiritual values on the shelf, succumbing to their fleshly desires over their spiritual need to obey and please God. Having sex with someone without being married can mess a dating relationship up, skewing a person's mental capacity, causing the sexual encounter to seriously affect your spiritual decision making capability. The EMOTIONAL ATTACHMENT during an unauthorized sexual encounter with someone whom you are not married to can IMMOBILIZE your RATIONALE to critically think about choosing a spiritual candidate for marriage. When two individuals fornicate, the pleasure that exists in the midst of a sexual encounter could easily give those involved a false emotional connection that never really existed as you can erroneously feel connected emotionally to someone because you've become intimate with them; but that doesn't mean they even like you or that you even like them.

The devil has a way of allowing lust to disguise itself as love and sometimes people don't even realize it. For some, sex is only about enjoying the pleasure of what someone gives them, how their physical desires are fulfilled, but that has nothing to do with loving that person as a Godly mate for marriage! One can enjoy the pleasure of sin and the devil can convince you that it's love when it's not, and you may never see that there really is no mutual love without the unauthorized premarital sexual relationship. The devil knows how to make you feel in love when you sin, but in actuality you were only in lust with the person. Unfortunately, for that matter many women and men have fallen victim to this kind of thinking and got hurt.

Most men know how to *attach* themselves to a woman sexually during the physical act of pleasure, but also know how to quickly *detach* themselves afterwards, feeling nothing emotionally, having the ability to walk away after sex, feeling no love connection at all, thus playing the woman emotionally. If you're dating someone hoping to get married one day, but you feel the need to sin by having sex with the person just to keep that person involved with you in the dating relationship, I suggest that you may want to rethink whether or not it's God that wants you to be with them or whether it's the enemy that does.

A good question to ask is who sent this person to me? Was it God or the enemy? Premarital sex can destroy hopeful SPIRITUAL RELATIONSHIPS and hinder SPIRITUAL MARRIAGES! If one person in a marriage is experienced, having been extremely sexually active prior to marriage, but the other hasn't, it's possible that the person with little or no prior sexual experiences may not have the ability to sexually perform at the level their spouse was previously accustomed to. Now, the relationship could seem rewarding and exhilarating for one person, but sexually unappealing or boring to the other. Premarital sexual activity could damage the marriage, resulting in the unsatisfied spouse seeking alternatives, such as watching pornography, committing adultery, becoming emotionally disengaged, leading to a lack of intimacy, thus ruining the relationship; but it all started through the sinful behavior displayed in the form of premarital sex.

I hope that the aforementioned behavior doesn't happen in any relationship; my point is that it can happen as PREMARITAL problems become MARITAL PROBLEMS. Doing things God's way gives you the confidence to know that God is leading the way and guiding you in your spiritual relationship in His direction. I'm not judging, but a consistency I see is that many spiritual people sometimes date the worldliest carnal-minded people. They consider themselves having fallen in love with them, marry them, and have a future expectation that over time that person will change. After some time later in the marriage, they realize that person isn't going to change so they become frustrated, contemplate leaving the marriage, separate or even decide to divorce. As a child of God, you cannot consciously marry a sinner and get mad when he or she practices sin during the marriage without having any intent to change, as though they never demonstrated or practiced any righteousness prior to marriage or displayed any Christian behavior before you married them.

Sadly, many people have false, lofty, and erroneous expectations for persons to behave spiritually in a marriage who never demonstrated any interest to behave spiritual in the dating relationship. I know women who married ungodly, non-church attending men, but they expected them to suddenly attend Church, and then become frustrated when the man shows no interest in attending Church years after they have been married. As a matter of fact, that brother hadn't been in the Church building since the day his wedding took place and for some reason that woman feels betrayed. The point is, if a man or woman never demonstrated any spiritual interest or consistent Christian practice in the dating phase, it would be foolish to expect it in the marriage or feel betrayed when you assumed things would change when they didn't. This should not be an indictment on the person who never committed to changing; rather the earnest must be on the person who expected this change to take place with someone who never committed to changing before they decided to marry you.

If you are currently having sex before marriage with a dating partner, simply have Godly sorrow for your sinful behavior and repent. (Acts 17:30-31; 1 Cor 6:9-11) You can furthermore improve your situation by terminating the sexual intimacy immediately. I know that other books, movies, and music have insinuated that it's okay to engage in sex after three months, but I must tell you, God doesn't endorse that notion at all. (1 Cor 6:9-11) *"Marriage is to be held in honor among all, and the marriage bed is to be undefiled; for fornicators and adulterers God will judge"* (Hebrews 13:4). A fornicator is one who engages into sexual immorality being sexually active as an unmarried person. The word fornicator comes from the original word *"pornos"* which is where we get the English word "porn or pornography" and it literally means to *"prostitute oneself,"* as one who unlawfully engages in sexual immortality. So, in terms of spiritual dating behavior, the unmarried person who wants to go to heaven, who abstains from the practice of fornication, has to decide whether they will listen to God or listen to man, who advocates for the practice of sex after a trial period without the covenant commitment of the marriage.

Let me tell you what started me on a path determined to find a spiritual relationship that reflects what I perceive as the best influence to find a mate. I learned that if a person knows God, then it would be easier for them to love me the way I need to be loved, because God is love and loves us unconditionally (1 John 4:19). What God demonstrates and displays is the very substance of Who He is, an unconditional sacrificial concept called love. What influenced me to love God and sacrifice my life for the cause of Christ is when I truly began to understand the love that God has for me and the sacrifice of His Son Jesus Christ. The unselfish, pure, sinless Son of God, died a cruel death being tormented, tortured, mocked, spat upon, whipped, and publically shamed to become the ransom for my sins, which God accepted for the atonement of my sins. (Mark 10:45; 1 Timothy 2:6) When I internalized the depth of my sins, the depth of God's love and His desire to forgive me of all I did, all I wanted was a deeper relationship with Christ and became willing to do anything for the God who loved me that way, which included changing my purpose and reason for dating, finding someone to marry whom I loved who could help me so that we could glorify Him together. *"We love, because He first loved us."* (1 John 4:19)

God doesn't bless mess.

We must remember that God doesn't bless mess, so I encourage you not to block your blessings or settle for a relationship that takes you away from God and closer to the enemy. The fact that you have already had sex doesn't mean you have a relationship death sentence because you could certainly find a qualified mate ultimately having a wonderful marriage and a powerful testimony, having terminated the practice of premarital sex. God just intended for sexual intimacy to come from the covenant of a marriage, not outside of the marriage bond. God's original design for mankind was sexual purity. For Adam and Eve, everything about their relationship was new and their sexual intimacy was new as well. There is something awesome about new things. We love new clothes, shoes, toys, cars, and houses. We just love new things and often anticipate the joy of what having new things provide.God's intent was for sexual intimacy to be new, for the purpose of physical enjoyment, emotional stimulation, pleasure and useful for procreation purposes for a husband and wife. Unfortunately when cohabitation is practiced, there is no new thrill, no anticipation of anything new and not much to look forward to in marriage. Consequently, marriage then lacks participants who view it as a higher level of commitment.

I'll never forget that day when I very enthusiastically congratulated a lady who had just gotten married but had the most uninterested facial expressions I may have ever seen, she said, *"We've been together for fifteen years and marriage is nothing but a piece of paper."* I thought to myself what a terrible way to view what God has created, but her experiences in cohabitating skewed her view about marriage, thus causing her not to view marriage with the honor God created it to have. (Heb 13:4) Marriage is a higher level of commitment than dating, it's a higher level of commitment than living together, and it's a higher level of commitment than being engaged. Marriage is a spiritual commitment with God as its participants both men and women are blessed to be joined together as one flesh with God, operating as the Glue that keeps the married persons together. (Gen 2:24)

Celebrating Celibacy

I know what it's like to spend many cold, lonely, and sleepless nights alone feeling sexually frustrated, it's called being human. However, it was worth it for me. If I had to do it all over again I would do it again in a heartbeat, knowing the blessings that God gives when His children seek to do what is right in His sight. After having sex before marriage as a young person I had sinned and broken myself from the purity God desires for husband and wife. I made up my mind that I wasn't going to allow lust, desire, and fleshly thoughts to encompass my mind, so I repented of my sins. I was celibate for five years before I was married. During those five years, I was able to understand why God wanted His people to remain virgins before marriage. **Celibacy is more than not just having intercourse, its finding spiritual strength to be satisfied with life through your relationship with Christ.** Likewise, in 2 Corinthians 12:10, Paul said, "*Therefore I am well content with weaknesses, with insults, with distresses, with persecutions, with difficulties, for Christ's sake; for when I am weak, then I am strong.*"

Some may think that it's impossible to have discovered the physical, then possess the power to abstain from it. Jesus Christ said, "*All things are possible to them who believe*" (Mk 9:23). In my life I came to the conclusion that if I was going to be blessed by God to find the wife He wanted for me, I could not be asking God for a wife or anything while practicing sin. I'll never forget a conversation my best friend and I were having about God that changed my life. We discussed how God had truly blessed us with our current level of behavior, knowing we both could do better and we talked about how if we fully turned our lives over to God, how much more blessed we would be. That conversation blessed me because too many people have consistently blocked their own blessings because they have not fully surrendered to the Savior. I believed that if Christ could die for me the way He died, having to suffer knowing I would be disobedient for all those years, sacrificing to abstain from fleshly desires was nothing to me anymore. I didn't care what friends, females or anybody thought as my conscience was forever branded, appreciating the sacrifice of Christ's blood so that I could be saved and forgiven. My point is that God can allow you the time and space as a single person to become front and center with Him. I'm reminded of that song by Michael W. Smith that says *"Here I am to worship; Here I am to bow down; Here I am to say that You're my God. You're all together lovely; Altogether worthy; Altogether wonderful to me."* Many people underestimate the power of the Holy Spirit to sustain your physical desires being satisfied spiritually until God blesses you to be satisfied physically with a spouse in marriage. There is a liberating feeling of being in control of your actions because of your relationship with Jesus. It is an indescribable feeling and only a blessing that God can give. I believe when you trust God with a made up mind not to settle for any relationship, God can bless you with the spiritual relationship both you and He desire for your life, undoubtedly one that will glorify Him!

Preventing Dating Slips By Utilizing Dating Tips

Physical attraction is real and should not be taken lightly. As a child of God, no matter how dedicated you are to the Lord, no matter how much you practice Christianity and love the Lord, anyone who gets themselves into a high pressure situation where both dating partners hormones are raging wild could easily get caught off guard by placing themselves into a spiritually compromising situation where they slip

35

up and commit a sexual sin. Whether you are a virgin or one who is practicing abstinence, it could happen to the best of us. Here are a few dating tips that will help prevent some dating slips that could lead to sin or an awkward relationship as a result of the aftermath of a sexual sin.

1) *Know yourself.* Here is a realistic dating scenario that can easily happen. Both the man and women dating each other are on the couch beside each other just talking and watching television. She gets sleepy and leans on him. Naturally he comforts her and places his arm around her and she gets more comfortable, now placing her head is on his shoulder. She looks up and he looks down having their faces so close together and without thinking about it the next thing you know they are kissing, touching, rubbing, releasing all the built up awkward sexual tension. Things could even progress further than kissing and both parties could lose sight on the fact that things are going in the wrong direction in a hurry. If you are like me and have made this mistake before, you need to know yourself and what you are capable of getting into and what you are capable of allowing to happen. Be honest about knowing what your tendencies and weaknesses are. Make sure you do not place yourself in positions where you have failed before and lost cognizance of what you are doing so that you don't participate in unhealthy relationship behaviors that either are sinful or ones that lead to sin.

2) *Offense is the best Defense.* Dating persons must become PROACTIVE instead of REACTIVE. In dating, the focus has to shift from carnal behavior to spiritual behavior. Carnal

Dating persons must become PROACTIVE *instead of* REACTIVE.

minded dating will always get you into trouble. You can better maintain your spiritual integrity when you display and demonstrate offensive dating behavior. Do not think you can merely rely on defending yourself once you have allowed yourself to be placed in a compromising high-pressure situation to sin. If you are familiar with the above example of dating in my first point, I showed you a couple being on the couch succumbing to the practice of physical intimacy that could lead to sexual sins like lust and fornication. You have to refuse placing yourself in that kind of position. Avoid the closeness on the couch and starring into someone's eyes or even looking at a person in a way that causes problems or intensifies the need or sensations which could lead to practicing sin. Avoid any kind of physical touch if you know it could hinder you from behaving becomingly as a child of God.

3) *Avoid Your Triggers* – Remember that the devil has never **made** anyone sin. All the enemy does is provide the demonic influence through various manipulative measures which we succumb to and we make the decision to sin. A drug dealer supplies and sales the poison, but he doesn't make you do the drugs, people do that. The enemy uses people, places, problems, predicaments, mindsets, lusts, drugs, alcohol, attraction, music, clothing, and even food which provide the influence for us to sin. Usually, when a fisherman goes out fishing he has a strategy to catch a certain kind of fish so he uses the bait that entices the fish because the experienced fisherman knows what has been attractive to lure the fish in the past. In your past, the enemy has watched you struggle with sin, he saw you give in to certain devices, strongholds and temptations, so he places what he knows is the most effective kind of bait, to lure you so that you will bite on it. You have to avoid the people, places and positions that serve as triggers for you to act unbecomingly as a child of God.

YOU CAN NOT surround yourself with the things that trigger you to sin and wonder why it is so tough to avoid temptation. If you find yourself involved in something that God is not pleased with just simply decide not to go any further. Take the spiritual high road and say NO or tell yourself or someone to STOP! I remember in college when I had an 8:00am class, we could see through the classroom windows who was walking from the girls dormitory or the boys dormitory back to their own dormitory and the students called it the "the walk of shame." The guilt of sin should serve as a powerful change agent for the child of God who knows better, and who is much better than the behavior they display at times. That kind of guilt can be eliminated if you follow the tips that will keep you from slipping and make up your mind to repent as repentance changes behavior and practices.

We all have natural desires, but when one has engaged in premarital sexual activity, you need to know that *marriage was not created or designed as a cover up institution just to cover up one's sins.* Some people simply use getting married to cover up the guilt of sins such as fornication, particularly when a woman gets pregnant during a dating courtship. We all would be wise to know that God gave His Son Jesus Christ as a sin Sacrifice, dying for our sins so that through faith, repentance, and baptism He would eliminate the practice of sin after believers are born again (Acts 2:36-47), but marriage wasn't created for people who do not love each other to cover up their guilt of their sin in a purposeless marriage. It has often been

Marriage was not created or designed as a cover up institution just to cover up one's sins.

said that two wrongs don't make a right. Marriage is simply a love union between husband and wife, a mutual commitment to each other and to God, to live in harmony with God.

Marriage is not something to enter into WITH ANYONE just because you have already slept with them or have children with them, knowing you have no compatibility. In 1 Corinthians 7:9 there is a passage that some people have misinterpreted, that has led many people down a path of marriage with the wrong person. *"But if they cannot contain, let them marry: for it is better to marry than to burn."* (1 Corinthians 7:9 KJV) The word "contain" comes from the original word *egkrateuomai* which means "to exercise self control." Because of the Christians in Corinth's inability to exercise self control, the Apostle Paul advised them to marry, so that they would not burn with passion. The word "burn" in context in 1 Corinthians 7:9 is not referring to being married as some urgent act to prevent burning as in burning in hell for having sexual desires, burn means "to set on fire" which refers to having ones ***sexual desires*** being set ablaze, which could lead a person to engage into a premarital sexual relationship before marriage, which is fornication (sin). Some have read this and concluded that since their hormones, physical attraction, and appetite for sexual activity is raging, they need to get married to avoid burning in hell for having those desires. In context, this passage addresses a larger issue that believers in Corinth had as they questioned whether it was good for a man to touch a woman. (1 Cor 7:1) The response the Apostle Paul wrote was *"But because of immoralities, each man is to have his own wife, and each woman is to have her own husband."* (1 Cor 7:2) It is certainly true, that having a spouse of the opposite sex helps fulfill desires for sexual intimacy for both husband and wife, as well as potentially preventing immorality in this context, but to be clear, Paul is giving the unmarried and widows the right to MARRY, but the text doesn't teach a person to just MARRY ANYBODY! (1 Cor 7:8) It doesn't mean marry someone that you aren't compatible with, someone whom you haven't dated long enough to know well enough to marry or even gotten a chance to know.

Lastly, it certainly doesn't mean marrying someone unspiritual, who may not love Jesus, who can't help you get to heaven, or marrying someone who may even prevent you from going to heaven. Heaven has to be the most important thing for believers to strive for, so placing yourself into an unhealthy relationship because you have made the mistake of having premarital sex as a child of God, should not be the reason one rushes into a marriage. The best thing to do is to repent and terminate the sexual intimacy within the dating relationship.

In a marriage it can also become emotionally draining and spiritually challenging to coexist under the same roof if marital participants share vast religious differences. God is love and we love because He first loved us (1 Jn 4:19). However, those who desire to honor God must date with a spiritual purpose, evaluating people to find out if the person possesses any spiritual complimentary behaviors that resemble what God would desire for a marriage. There have been countless times where I've experienced both men and women seemingly trapped, enduring the tumultuous pain of relationships that cause them so much stress, anxiety, tears,

Paul is giving the unmarried and widows the right to MARRY, but the text doesn't teach a person to just MARRY ANYBODY!

and trouble that in reality never had a chance to work from the beginning. One of the primary reasons I wanted to write this book was to help those people who have experienced those kinds of relationships, who still desire to be married, to begin to date with a spiritual purpose, investigating the spiritual side of God's way in their next dating relationship going forward.

I remember having a conversation with a young lady who was a previously divorced professional providing for her family but had been in bad relationship after bad relationship. I would frequently hear her say that her boyfriend would come over to spend the night. She would complain saying that he never wants to go out anywhere to spend any time with her during the daytime. I replied, "Really, how long have you been dating?" She replied, "Five years." I responded and said, "Any hopes for marriage?" She replied, "We've never really talked about it because he still hasn't made a commitment to me yet, but I believe he will one day because he loves me." Wow! She was oblivious and so naïve to the fact that this man was using her simply to sleep with her and never had any intentions on doing anything else, but stringing her along just to get what he wanted. This is just one of many examples of how dating without a purpose can waste valuable time off your life that you can never get back and all you have to show for it is a broken heart, embarrassment, and a feeling that you have been taken advantage of, having lost some of the best years of your life.

Practice

On May 7, 2002, NBA Superstar Allen Iverson, point guard for the Philadelphia 76er's, conducted an interview where he was asked about practice after a game in a press conference by a reporter and he was quoted saying, *"Practice? We're talking about Practice? Not a game but were talking about PRACTICE!"* This reminded me of my mindset as a

Christian, not just a Preacher, but a Christian, because each day we have to practice our beliefs in our moral behavior and be examples to the world in Christianity. Even though going to church is good, I didn't want to marry someone simply on the basis of them attending church, because many people attend church, but have no intentions of ever practicing Christianity. Although, I believe in faith, repentance and that baptism for the remission of sins is essential to salvation, I didn't want to marry a person just on the basis of them having been baptized and being a member of the church. (Acts 2:38,41) I wanted to marry a person who practiced Christianity consistently. Too many times I've seen people enter into marriage thinking that things would be different at some point. Consequently, some spouses never live up to those expectations. To marry a person expecting them to be different and more spiritual or to even become a Christian isn't guaranteed. Once you decide to get married you have to make up your mind to be comfortable with the amount of Christianity that person either has or has not displayed RIGHT NOW! Many people have made erroneous external indictments on a marriage spouse who they, themselves had unmerited expectations for that were never warranted. The question is whether you are willing to take the time it takes to find a person who is actively practicing Christianity.

Proverbs 18:22 says, *"He who finds a wife finds a good thing And obtains favor from the LORD."* There is much wisdom in that text. The man who finds a wife undoubtedly has found a "good thing." What's fascinating is that the text teaches what God calls "good." Finding a wife is

I wanted to marry a person who practiced Christianity consistently.

a good thing, a blessing, not some bad, arduous, troubling experience. The text doesn't specifically say how the finding of a wife occurs which could be in a multiplicity of ways. The premise is that when a wife is found by the husband, he has found something that is good. Then the question becomes how does finding a wife help a man obtain favor from the Lord? The word "favor" means grace (unmerited favor), acceptability and goodwill, obtained by the husband, from the Lord when a wife is found. Sometimes, the favor the husband receives from God is certainly that which he doesn't deserve from the Lord. (Prov 18:22) For what husband in all his imperfections has earned the right for someone to love them unconditionally, care for them during sickness, tolerate their ignorance, accept their past mistakes and in many cases, stand with them when many other wives would leave because the circumstances became so overwhelming? That's why having a wife is a good thing, it can only be given to a man by God, from Whom favor was obtained and given to the husband. (Prov 18:22) The very idea of not loving your God-given good thing would be disrespectful to the Creator, with Whom the husband found the favor to obtain a good thing. At the point of the marriage bond, God's favor is attained without merit and the Lord's favor must be maintained through the husband's love for his wife, his good thing. (Prov 18:22; Eph 5:22)

The bible doesn't mention much about dating, but it says much about marriage as God wants His people to

Finding a wife is a good thing, a blessing, not some bad, arduous, troubling experience.

become united with Him in marriage as one flesh, as God is the Author of marriage. Marriage must involve the man, the woman, and God as the Glue that unites and keeps the couple together. (Gen 2:23-24; Heb 13:4) If God isn't the Focus of the relationship, then what are the factors and forces that govern how the relationship operates? Unfortunately, many times people desire to participate in a husband and wife relationship and become joined in what the Word of God defines as marriage, but the problem is many people get married and never operate in the marriage dynamic the way the Creator of marriage designed it to operate. How can we participate in what God has created (marriage), but never exhibit the kind of behavior in that marriage that is according to His Word and then expect it to work? I remember I learned this concept the hard way. A garment of clothing I owned specified how it needed to be cleaned with a tag saying, do not wash, dry clean only. You know the rest of that story. I destroyed the garment because I refused to follow the instructions from the manufacturer of how to correctly clean it. God is the only One who can clean your marriage and His instructions guide us on how to keep our marriages clean. Being in a marriage, but not doing what God, the Creator of marriage, says is like having a Mercedes Benz and complaining about it never working properly, when you have replaced all the factory parts with Chevrolet parts, having the nerve to take it to every other mechanic, except the Mercedes Benz manufacturer, the actual creator of the vehicle to diagnose or fix it. Many people do the same thing in dating relationships. They choose to receive their relationship advice, answers, and influences from music, unspiritual people and friends who have been unsuccessful in purpose driven dating themselves, instead of going to God, the Creator of marriage. You cannot display and demonstrate unspiritual behavior, which leads to the practice of sin, then expect the marriage to flourish, having no sign of God involved in it. God tells us the behavior He desires for spouses to operate in the marriage bond. (Eph 5:22-33; Col 3:18-21; 1 Pet 3:1-7) If two people are in a relationship with one person committed and the other uncommitted that relationship will constantly be an uphill battle full of ups and downs just to stay together, with happiness so infrequent or never a consistent reality.

The number one goal of a Christian is to make it to heaven! Relationships MUST be viewed with your #1 goal in mind otherwise you can be blinded by the attractiveness and physicality of a mate, the emotional feeling of belonging and being with someone and the enticing lure of desiring not to be alone. For the Christian, dating must be a measured, calculated, prayed about phenomenon where candidates are determined and choices are made based on the spiritual value a person has right now, not in the future. ***Expectations have unfortunately caused many to make unwise decisions to get into long term relationships with people who have only displayed short term potential.*** If you truly want to go to heaven, ask yourself the question, can this person help me get there?

Years ago, I remember hearing a gospel Preacher named Harold Redd say, "The goal of a man is to get his family to heaven." That statement never left my mind and deeply impacted my thinking. I frequently pose this question to singles that are dating who say they want to go to heaven. If you really want to go to heaven, why marry someone who has no desire to go or presently couldn't help you get there? I love evangelism, helping and teaching people the value of coming to Jesus Christ to be saved, but I've learned that you don't have to marry someone to evangelize to them. You can simply

"The goal of a man is to get his family to heaven."

expose them to the Word of God and let God convict them. Expecting a change once you marry a person could never come to fruition. Your love for God and being obedient to the Lord MUST be the reason you make decisions in choosing someone to marry. The spiritual purpose of dating is to sift through candidates for marriage through many conversations as friends to determine who you should take seriously as a candidate for marriage and to see who qualifies for you to marry. The good news is that if that friend doesn't have what you desire as a mate for marriage, then you have simply gained a friend who may be a great asset in your life for quite a long time if you have kept the relationship plutonic. If getting married is what you want, then your purpose in dating someone is simply to evaluate potential candidates to see if they are someone you could marry and work with to go heaven together as one flesh in Christ Jesus.

STUDY GUIDE

Below is a list of **<u>FIVE THINGS</u>** every single person who wants to be married should know and do in dating with a spiritual purpose and will help avoid being too thirsty.

1) **Make a list.** Write down all the character traits you would like to have in a spouse, things you aren't willing to compromise on, but those things need to be realistic. Example: Being a practicing Christian, desire for family, effective communicator, open mindedness, non-smoker, effective money manager, purpose driven, spiritual attraction, physical attraction, caring heart, good personality and strong work ethic, etc. If your list of qualities you desire is not realistic, then realistically you're being unrealistic about human beings thus limiting your true chances of finding the person for your life. Example: *I want to be with someone who works out 5 days a week for 45 minutes.* There is nothing wrong with that demand at all, but if you're not doing those things yourself how can you expect it of someone else? Also, is that expectation you have something you are willing to allow to be a deal breaker? If so, it's fine, just realize you have only created a smaller myopic pool of dating candidates to choose from.

2) **Ask 21 Questions.** Questions are powerful. A question can divulge much needed information in dating that can help you make wise, spiritual decisions as to whether you should seriously consider them as a potential candidate for marriage. Get used to and comfortable with asking questions. If asking someone a question messes up the courtship, praise the Lord! Now you can see how God reveals what He intended for you to know through a question, which gave you

insight that you needed to know about that person's intent, life, attitude, and overall understanding on the topic you asked them just because you asked someone a question. You have to get to know people and verbal communication is a major factor in doing that. Verbal communication through the avenue of talking and asking questions will illicit verbal communicative responses. You MUST develop the ability to tell whether or not someone is simply running game on you. Asking open ended questions forces people to discuss important things in detail, exposes those who can or cannot articulate answers or describe experiences when they communicate with you. If a person cannot answer simple open-ended questions with sincerity, giving you a genuine response, then you need not overlook the fact that this person could either be lying, have issues communicating or doesn't have the qualities you desire. You cannot afford to allow yourself to be blinded by the potential of the successful long term courtship. So many times people allow themselves to be blinded by the relationships potential, a person's physical appearance or swagger, thus losing relationship sight, becoming blinded, consequently missing all the warning signs of someone who doesn't qualify as a spiritual mate for marriage.

3) **Avoid Getting Emotionally Connected Too Fast.** We live in a technological world where almost everything is online. I've seen many people fall in love online before they ever physically met a person. There are many success stories and even marriages that initially began

You cannot afford to allow yourself to be blinded by the potential of the successful long term courtship.

when people met online, but there are much more horror stories that happen from online dating and internet connections. I would warn everyone not to invest any emotional energy into someone they haven't physically seen or met in person. In this day and age a single person, young and old, MUST ***Become Aware of Online Romance Scams.*** In other words, every day the number of victims from online dating scams are increasing. Unfortunately, hackers create fake online user profiles and use real pictures of other people and disguise themselves as that person making up lies to develop relationships with people to ultimately scam them. If you have an online profile on a social media site that lists yourself as single, unmarried, widowed, divorced or even married YOU might be a target for these professional scam artists. They target the lonely, single, weak, widowed, wearied, vulnerable, and hurting people every day. So before you get excited about a new dating prospect from another state, city, town or country, please understand that person may not even be the real person they are projecting themselves as. Scam artists prey on the disparity and vulnerability of lonely single people in order to extract money using tactics, tools, and technology to make things seem so real just to convince people they are legitimate, getting them to believe in a cockamamie lie just to send or wire them money. Beware of investing time, energy, effort and emotional feelings into a person who you don't know.

Beware of investing time, energy, effort and emotional feelings into a person who you don't know.

4.) **Be Friends.** Establish a plutonic friendship with boundaries as simply friends, not friends with benefits.

It's okay to have friends of the opposite sex if there is a mutual understanding between both parties that the relationship is strictly a friendship with no romantic attachment. Labeling someone as a dating partner too soon can be a mistake, but labeling someone as a friend and having the same definition of what a friend is in most cases should guard against the notion that the friendship is more than what it is. It would be a great idea to discuss what a friendship is before you spend too much time with a person because they could have differing definitions of dating in contrast to your definition of dating. Some people have a traditional dating value system and believe in only dating one person at a time, but most people with a traditional dating mindset believe that it's okay to have more than one friend so you're probably on safe ground if you establish a real friendship, making sure that everyone is on the same page as to what "being friends" means and how that kind of friendship operates.

5.) **Pray for Confirmations from God.** There are many things in dating relationships that the Lord has to reveal to you, but that may not happen if you have not prayed to God about blessing you with the right person. Your prayer to God should consist of asking Him to open your eyes, showing you what you need to see, which includes the good, the bad and the ugly. God has to give you spiritual insight to ask the right questions, giving you the ability to look deeper than the surface of a conversation. God has to confirm things for you as you date. Has God ever given you a confirmation on something important that you obeyed or ignored? Compare the outcome of when you ignored God's confirmation about something versus when you acted upon His confirmations. God has a unique way of giving spiritual confirmations to show us things if we pay close attention.

God sometimes gives confirmations through people, reoccurrences, and visual confirmations through consistent or inconsistent behaviors of people and most importantly through His Word. If you remain in prayer for confirmations in the dating process, when you noticeably experience consistent behavior that is the opposite of God's will, that is certainly confirmation that God doesn't approve of it. Likewise if the confirmation points to a positive behavior outlined in God's will, then it confirms God does approve of that particular behavior. Remember, God is interested in making things work that benefit Him, His purpose and His will. God has the right to know what He will get out of the deal. If He blesses you with someone Godly, what are you going to do for God if He gives you an angel? Your response to what you are going to do for God together with this person makes a world of difference in the discovery phase of the dating relationship. I've said this before and it worked for me and my wife, God knows how to confirm to you who, when, what, and how He wants you to be in a relationship, and He has a way of revealing that to you. God knows you better than you know yourself and knows about your skepticism, your past, your flaws and the issues you have, as your Heavenly Father knows dating persons need spiritual confirmations. Let God lead in your dating process and pray without ceasing throughout the process (1 Thes 5:18).

God has the right to know what He will get out of the deal.

CHAPTER 5

The Blessing in the Breakup

T he truth is breakups can be very hurtful. It's frustrating being betrayed by someone with whom you wanted to make things work. To feel rejected, treated less than a person, and even manipulated is tough to swallow, but a truism for many people who have experienced a dating breakup or loss of a relationship. Some people have experienced life in a relationship which seemed to only amount to a lot of wasted time, tolerating immature, foolish behavior, lies, deceit, and jealousy. For those of you who desire to get married, you of all people understand how tough it is at times to be lonely, yearning for God to bless you with the person you desire for your life.

I've experienced many ups and downs in dating relationships having myself been hurt and unfortunately hurt others in the dating process as well. In the past I said to myself, this is the one! Then God helps you realize that person wasn't the one for you. It's not easy when you have invested time, energy, money, effort and most importantly EMOTION into a dating relationship that you hoped would end up in marital bliss, only to end

The truth is breakups can be very hurtful.

the dating relationship with a breakup where you sever any future hopes for marriage.

The good news is that there is a blessing in every breakup! You couldn't see it initially because you were emotionally invested so deeply into the relationship, to the degree that some people even think they will never get back to the point of being so close to being married again. At some point we all must learn that God can use every breakup to become a bridge to get you closer to the person that the Lord ultimately has for your life. Sometimes breakups occur because someone could not see the value and worth you possessed which has in hindsight become a blessing because one's dating farsightedness would also be detrimental to the stability and longevity of a future marriage. What appear to be failed dating relationships are really stepping stones and necessary life events for some people as those relationships can teach you much about what you will or will not be able to tolerate in a marriage. If you can't tolerate certain things in someone's behavior while dating, it's best to learn that early in the courtship, rather than finding it out later in the marriage.

There are powerful life lessons in every seemingly unsuccessful dating relationship that strategically teach its participants valuable lessons that will help those who date become better prepared, stronger, more knowledgeable, and mature for the person God may desire to put into someone's life. Many times, God allows single persons to experience dating relationships (breakups) so that you can learn some things about yourself. Everyone has baggage and imperfections, but it's always easier to see faults in everybody else but yourself! If you took a metaphorical dating microscope and looked back, combing through some of your past dating relationships could it be that you could have been a better listener, displayed more patience, flexibility, availability and been less unselfish? If your relationship did not end with a breakup, who is to say that you would have ever learned anything about your own personal insecurities, faults, issues, quirks, and qualms? Breakups are very much needed because they generate opportunities for self-assessment. The problem with some singles is they jump into relationship after relationship still hurt from the last relationship, because they don't want to feel alone, consequently never allowing for time to heal, grow, and self-reflect. Marriage takes work and requires both participants to be emotionally healthy, ready to fight for each other and the marriage. No spouse desires to fight on the marriage battlefield with an emotionally wounded soldier. Naturally, those who haven't taken the time to heal take the same baggage into every relationship and in many cases, drift from relationship to relationship, never realizing they ruin every new relationship before it even gets started which I discussed more in-depth in the chapter, "Dating Under the Influence," in the section titled, "The Satire of Relationship Sabotage." This book "Finding My Good Thing," will challenge your thinking and provide knowledge to help you understand that breakups are okay and you don't have to worry about being alone as sometimes God successfully uses a season of loneliness to become a season of preparation when He allows you to experience self-reflection so that you can become prepared for the person whom He ultimately has for your life. As a single person, if you know you're not in a space or place to maintain a healthy relationship, you must process that difficult truth. If God gave you the right person of your dreams during the wrong time in your life you probably couldn't even see it or you may even mess it up because there is something within you that must be addressed before you can truly offer THE BEST YOU.

You may not see it now, but at some point in this book I hope that you praise God for every relationship that you thought "failed." As a single person you have to change your perception of relationships which did not end in a marriage or that ended even in cancelled engagements because some relationships never really fail as we perceive them to. They become relationships through which God "reveals" things to you. I call these REVELATIONSHIPS. Dating relationships that end without the future of romance and marriage "reveal" truth and knowledge about the reality of the kinds of relationships we all need or do not need. Those realities are sometimes hurtful to realize, those relationship realities may even make you cry and some of those realities are designed to humble you. The end of a dating relationship could be one of the best blessings God gives you outside of salvation because the reality is, the ending of a relationship could be God saving you from a lifetime of pain, a lifetime of misery, a lifetime of hurt and a lifetime of asking WHY? Okay! If you really believe God has used past relationship to develop you for your future mate for marriage why don't you STOP right now in the middle of reading this chapter and take a five second PRAISE BREAK of thanksgiving being thankful to God for blessing you with all of your past REVELATIONSHIPS! Don't misinterpret the hard core truths that past, prior or previous dating relationships were designed to actually reveal relational truth for you to learn from.

Revelationships

The problem with dating relationships is that we perceive they failed instead of perceiving the value of what they reveal about our decision making within those relationships. It's easy to allow the

They become relationships through which God "reveals" things to you. I call these REVELATIONSHIPS.

enemy to negatively impact your thinking towards having a successful future dating relationship which ends in a holy marriage, if you do not view past relationships as REVELATIONSHIPS from your past.

Have you been around a scared and emotionally wounded person who says, "I tried marriage before once and it didn't work so I'll never get married again?" Or you may have heard a brother or sister say, "I've been lied on, cheated on, hurt, taken advantage of and let down by people too many times, so marriage isn't for me." So many people are hurt and adamantly oppose the idea of marriage because of the practical outcome they experienced in previous marriages or relationships and honestly it's understandable. However, you should never let your past experiences, as negative as they may have been, to cause you to ever limit God. When a person limits God, it shows that they have a limited understanding of God. God is too powerful to be understood fully, too Complex to be constrained or to be categorized by the control or thinking of human wisdom. Too many good men and women have allowed relationships that ended on bad terms to change their desire to be married when God really blessed them to have a REVELATIONSHIP. Your past relationships were merely intended to bring out the best in you! Those realities should bring out the best of your thinking, the best of your desire to love, the best in your personality, the best in your strength and willpower to succeed, even against your hurtful experiences. Don't paint every man or every woman with the same brush and don't give up on finding your good thing that is really out there for you to meet, which will give you a testimony that I am a witness to in my own life

When a person limits God, it shows that they have a limited understanding of God.

having experienced hurt through trials, but ended in triumph. Because your relationship ended the way it did, it may simply expose a deeper reality that many people miss seeing throughout the dating relationship or chose to ignore, which came back to finish the relationship off.

Since your last relationship ended, God needs to reveal something to you that you need to know before you get into a new relationship, but you need to dig deep into the relationship at some point to access what really happened. I can vividly remember while I played basketball at Emerald High School in Greenwood, SC and for Newberry College that the coaches made us watch film before and after we played opposing teams. When we watched film before we played a team, we studied their plays, examined the positions certain players played, searched for weaknesses as well as evaluated their strengths. After watching much game film, the coaches developed a game plan, a strategy to be successful to win the games before we even played opposing teams. After we played a team win or lose we watched film to see what we did wrong, what we did good; we explored ways to improve, and so should it be with dating relationships. So many times people date without a strategy; they just date with no deliberate intent to know specific things about the person, failing to properly view the person's behavior, omitting pertinent details of their weaknesses and choosing to only see their strengths. Usually when a poorly executing basketball team devoid of structure, free lances the entire game, failing to run their plays, the team with the higher basketball IQ and structure will annihilate them because one team had a game plan and the other didn't. In dating if you have no game plan, someone with some game has already planned to run all over you and take whatever they want leaving you in the dust as you never saw it coming because you didn't properly execute a plan to date with a purpose.

Benjamin Franklin once said, "if you fail to plan, you have planned to fail." And Winston Churchill said, "Those who fail to learn from the past are doomed to repeat it." Relationships should challenge the participants to evaluate both sides of the dating coin, their perspective and your perspective. Look back at the relationship through the lenses of it being a REVELATIONSHIP. Could you have noticed some warning signs that something was wrong much earlier? Did you dismiss important character flaws? How much did your spirituality play in evaluating if that person was a spiritual fit for marriage? Did your spirituality play the biggest part in staying in the relationship? Were you behaving like you should have? Did you display the real you and did you allow your full personality to be displayed? One thing many people do is hold back expressing the full measure of who they are to someone because of fear. Fear cripples your thinking; it casually corrupts your character, causing a catastrophic conundrum to the existing complex conditions, confusing your critique of your dating companion with clutter. If you want to be married you have to put something into the process of dating to reach the end point, to find that special someone for your life. If you are hurt and emotionality bruised and it has effected your desire to put the effort into dating, to discern, decipher, and determine who is a good fit for you in dating, there is nothing wrong with working on yourself through the personal development that the Word of God offers, so that eventually you are in a position to receive what God has for you, being ready to give of yourself fully and completely.

Remember, the possibility of getting hurt by someone or being blinded by

How much did your spirituality play in evaluating if that person was a spiritual fit for marriage?

things will always be there, that's why you need the Holy Spirit to help guide you through the dating process. Moreover, God knows how to reveal to you who you can put yourself out there with in terms of exposing the real you. Personally, I would have rather gotten hurt, giving someone an opportunity to understand the real me than exude a protected scared version of myself that doesn't act, sound, behave, and accurately reflect the person who God made me to be. I AM me! Take it or leave it and that is the kind of attitude which shows trust in God's ability to give you someone who can accept you for who you really are. In the academic world, as Ministers of the Word, we Preachers have to exegete the Word of God to determine the meaning of the text so that we do not bring a predetermined meaning or interpretation to the text; we have to allow the text to interpret itself as we uncover the author's intended meaning. This process is called exegesis, when the reader studies to bring out (exegete) what the author intended to convey in the text, from the original authors point of view. We use hermeneutics, methods for interpreting scripture to bring out (exegesis) the biblical meaning of God's Word. Likewise each dating participant must have a dating hermeneutic to interpret what things actually mean in dating relationships. Get out your metaphoric dating shovels and dig deep into how things could have been better in your last few relationships so that in the next dating scenario you use what you dug up from the last relationship to be better prepared for the next one. Remember, some of the things you dig up need to remain permanently buried, you just need to exhume those things for research and educational purposes so that you try to never allow those things to surface again in future relationships.

Decisions

For the most part in Western culture and society, marriages in modern times are not arranged; they simply begin with a decision. Remember, if you were in a relationship that ended, ultimately it was your decision to be in that relationship. YOU chose that person to be in a dating or marital relationship with, so if it didn't work out, nobody made you date or marry them, but YOU! REVELATIONSHIPS teach us that we, of first importance, need to evaluate our decisions of who we choose with much more diligence and with a spiritual fine tooth comb. However, unfortunately many people simply choose to engage in a prosecutorial indictment on the institution of marriage itself, in their frustration in dealing with people in relationships as if God made them or forced them to date or marry someone that wasn't the right person for them. Sometimes it's not dating itself or marriage itself that really hurts us, it's the decision YOU MADE to be with the wrong person that ultimately led to a suffering relationship.

Decisions are powerful and should not be taken lightly when a person has to make one as we all have made good decisions and poor decisions that we regretted in the past. One decision could bless your life, or one decision could feel like there is a curse on your life when in actuality the curse is simply the lasting impact of one bad decision. God used the prophet Nathan to tell David the King about the repercussions of his sin, *"Now therefore, the sword shall never depart from*

One decision could bless your life, or one decision could feel like there is a curse on your life when in actuality the curse is simply the lasting impact of one bad decision.

your house, because you have despised Me and have taken the wife of Uriah the Hittite to be your wife.' (2 Sam 12:10) David made a decision to commit adultery, to plot, plan and prioritize having an innocent man's wife, having him murdered, thus violating God's Word, giving the enemies of the Lord occasion to blaspheme. (2 Sam 12:14) In this example, making that initial bad decision to sleep with Bathsheba, another man's wife, cost David a lifetime of pain and started a domino effect, a chain reaction, which plagued David for the rest of his life. (2 Sam 12:10) If you plan to be married, the decision of which person you choose to marry is arguably the second most powerful decision you will make in your life outside of becoming a Christian, a born again child of God.

Finally, the beauty of evaluating past REVEALATIONSHIP's after learning of your folly or other's foolishness, is the fact that God loves you and you still have the ability to get it right. When you can honestly take what God has revealed to you about yourself and others whom you have dated, the Lord can still lead you to the person He has for your life if you date with a spiritual purpose. The next time you date, use that opportunity to discover whether this person can aid, assist, and assimilate your journey to heaven RIGHT NOW, if not, he or she may not be what and who God wants for your life.

STUDY GUIDE

1) Assess whether you have consistently made spirit led decisions in choosing who you would date in your past breakups. Spend as much time as you need to think about some of your decisions to date certain people and what really influenced your decision to date them.

2) Engage in a conversation with a trusted spiritual confidant or other singles in a small group forum to discuss the importance of seeking to date people who are spiritual and how making wise decisions to date this way, using past experiences as evidence of why dating with a spiritual purpose is so important. Have each person list at least one spiritual quality that they will seek in a mate for marriage that they had previously not sought after or considered in past dating relationships. Make sure that your goal of obtaining someone with particular spiritual characteristics is something you consistently display yourself, which honors God.

3) Make a list of three BEHAVIORS that you DISPLAYED which honored God in past REVELATIONSHIP's, but you could improve on. Start TODAY making consistent efforts to improve in displaying those behaviors in all areas of your life to honor God TODAY.

4) Make a list of three BEHAVIORS that you DID NOT DISPLAY which could have honored God in past REVELATIONSHIP's that you seek to improve on. Start TODAY making consistent efforts to improve in displaying those behaviors in all areas to honor God.

CHAPTER 6

The Importance of Communication in Dating

I grew up in the 90's and I love tasteful R & B love music. One of my favorite R & B groups even to this day is Boyz II Men. In their song titled, "Water Runs Dry," the lyrics are *"We don't even talk anymore, and we don't even know what we argue about, don't even say I love you no more and saying how we feel is no longer allowed….."* It is a true statement that if there is no communication in a dating relationship or marriage, not only has the water run dry, the relationship is dry and that relationship needs to be baptized in communication in the name of love. **RELATIONSHIPS DEVOID OF COMMUNICATION AREN'T HEALTHY.**

A while back I spoke to an older successful gentleman who had recently overcome an illness, but had a lengthy hospital stay. He told me, "I never knew my wife was that sweet!" I said, "that's awesome Sir, but why do you say that?" The man said, "my wife took care of me while I was hospitalized which gave us an opportunity to have a meaningful conversation and it felt like it was the first time we had ever talked in a long time." I thought to myself, "wow, that's awesome, but why haven't they

Relationships devoid of communication aren't healthy.

conversed like that recently?" Then it dawned on me that this couple has been married for decades, but had no meaningful recent conversations where they both could appreciate the simplicity of what God blessed them with, each other. Furthermore, I wondered to myself how many couples are in marriage relationships, living together, but refuse to speak to each other, failing to communicate, secretly dying on the inside every day, passionately and emotionally longing for a social connection with the one whom they are supposed to be joined with together by God, living in the very house with a stranger. We are all human and this breakdown could easily happen to anyone in any relationship if no one is the catalyst in initiating the conversation. Have you been in a relationship or a marriage with someone who feels like a stranger? Why spend a lifetime with someone you don't even know?

Some people are miserable, aggravated and agitated in relationships with people who have negative, pessimistic, joyless attitudes, and behave as if they genuinely dislike each other, treating each other horribly. Jesus said, *"Treat others the same way you want them to treat you"* which includes husbands and wives. (Luke 6:31) Why can't those people get along? Did they not know that their spouse did those aggravating things in the dating process? Could they have at least asked some questions to see if the person could verbalize the reason for some of their beliefs, bitterness, and behaviors? I must admit that it is impossible to know everything in the dating process and about the person whom you date; usually the person you marry differs over time from the person you dated, as people change. When that change is good, it's called growth, and this positive change is conducive to producing a fruitful healthy spiritual relationship. In a marriage people must learn to adapt to new changes and challenges, but that's life. Even in sports, all good teams learn to make adjustments to get their teams to play at an optimum level, so healthy marriages must operate in the same manner.

Unfortunately, in dating relationships, some people are masterminds at masking themselves, showing almost undetectable unspiritual behavior while dating. Then they perform a bait and switch from the dating relationship to the marriage relationship, becoming completely different people than they were in the beginning. I've seen people stay in those relationships and spend their lives trying to reconcile, but I've also seen many of those kinds of relationships dissolve. Though this has sadly been a reality for many, it shows how important asking questions and evaluating behaviors are in the dating process. What gives dating hopefuls the best chance at finding a committed mate for marriage is to evaluate prospects spiritually, ASKING LOTS OF QUESTIONS, examining them, discovering if they consistently display spiritual behavior, as a practicing child of God. Maya Angelou said, "When someone shows you who they are, believe them." I would like to amplify and revise that powerful statement by saying, when someone shows you who they are with unacceptable behavior, not only should you believe them, don't marry them, unless you want to have a tumultuous marriage.

It's interesting that when we make major purchases such as houses and cars, we ask lots of questions, we purchase what we like, we assess the value of the property or vehicle we intend to purchase and get a thorough inspection and appraisal, before we decide to purchase anything. But for some reason, many people get into marriage relationships with a person, never ask any tough questions, refuse to receive any premarital counseling, operate under the false assumption that things will just work out and then wonder why the relationship is so tough to sustain. Unfortunately, some place more effort and due diligence into purchasing tangible assets than they place in getting to know a future lifetime marital companion. **Some people spend more time planning the wedding, than they spend getting to get know the person they plan to wed.** If the relationship lacks communication in the dating phase then the communication gap will quadruple in the marriage. Without someone stepping up to the plate and discussing the things that really matter, something that is small, tiny and myopic in the grand scheme of the relationship can escalate into something colossal if couples don't effectively communicate. Some men and women aren't expressive and do not feel comfortable expressing their feelings about their preferences, issues, habits and desires. But these are still things that need to be recognized upfront and verbally expressed in the dating process so that you can determine if you can work together to uncover solutions, overcoming these communicative dilemmas displaying a willingness to work towards effectively getting through those communication barriers. In John Maxwell's book called "Everyone Communicates Few Connect," he discusses effective ways to communicate, which is paramount in a relationship if you plan to spend the rest of your life with someone.

It is not wise to have the desire to be married and never discuss and communicate with each other all the important things and details that actually promote healthy marriages. I've asked people who didn't want to do marriage counseling, "who is going to pay the bills once you guys get married?" "Oh, we will figure it out." **FINANCES are IMPORTANT TO THE HEALTH OF A MARRIAGE!** No progressive minded brother or sister wants to eat bologna sandwiches for their entire marriage. Furthermore, complete financial disclosure in the dating phase is paramount. Expanding the family with children, saving for emergencies, putting children through school, participating in extracurricular activities, going on vacations and just paying the bills are all necessary conversations between dating persons that need to be transparent and honest. A lack of disclosure about money, credit, and any association with other outside financial responsibilities and obligations could damage, destroy, and be the detriment of the marriage, if not communicated clearly and understood by both parties during the dating process.

Blended Families

Blended family dynamics require work, desire, humility, and commitment, for the husband and wife to be on the same page for them to work. I've seen a lack of preparation, planning and patience, in the dating process, destroy marriages with blended families, but I've also seen them work beautifully. Without communication to plan and revise plans to make the daily family dynamic of a blended family work, things could be more challenging and become overwhelmingly difficult to deal with. *Communication is the key.* If you are dating and one person or both persons have children already, full disclosure about everything is crucial if you find someone you are interested in marrying. I've seen many blended family relationships suffer because of a lack of communication in regard to parenting the children. It takes two parents being on the same page about everything to work. Is there a connection with the future step parent and the step child in the dating relationship, or does hostility or tension exist? If you were to become married into a blended family, what are your expectations for raising the children together? How is each step parent going to discipline the adolescent, teenager, or grown step child, and are you comfortable with that? **WHAT ARE THE HOUSEHOLD RULES, WHO ENFORCES THEM, AND TO WHAT DEGREE ARE THESE RULES ENFORCED?** When you get married into a blended family, you are

Communication is the key.

marrying that person, joined together with God, but you are also now connected with everything and everyone that comes with the person you marry in the blended family dynamic. Their praises become your praises, but their problems also become your problems. Only God can keep blended families together and tight with one another. Without the Lord, blended or not blended, it will be difficult for people in marriages to forgive, let go and faithfully move on from issues. Every dating relationship needs to factor God into it and every marriage has to have God in it to survive, strive and remain successful.

Marriages Need Intimacy

Have you ever been around someone and you noticed that something wasn't right and after asking them what's wrong, they shy away from communicating as their frustration with the situation prevents them from communicating? Maybe, the reason is that person may have never developed the ability to communicate their hurts or to express their feelings in a civilized way that doesn't feel like an attack making the recipient respond defensively. Even though those people may not have verbally communicated or expressed their feelings, in actuality they are still communicating that something is wrong and they are unable to communicate the matter at that time. A lack of communication in the dating phase metastasizes in a marriage, thus negatively impacting the ability to deepen the intimacy that both the husband and wife need. Intimacy in a marriage is like having a luxury car with no gas in it, without gas, you're not going anywhere. Communication, whether verbal or non-verbal, creates those good internal positive feelings we need to connect with each other and that creates intimacy.

One of my biggest pet peeves is when married folks talk negatively about their spouse, display silence around their spouse or take pleasure in willingly communicating to someone else what they refuse to communicate to the very person they were joined together with as one flesh (Gen 2:24). NEVER talk about your spouse negatively even if what you may say about them is 100% true. The only time you should ever talk about your spouse to anyone else is when you are lifting them up and singing their praises. **Because when a married person negatively talks about their spouse, technically they're talking about themselves as well because they are ONE flesh!** Failure to positively communicate respectfully toward a spouse is oxymoronic, as the one who talks negatively about their spouse should realize they were the person who decided to choose that spouse, which speaks volumes about their decision making ability, standards and relationship acumen! Nobody spends money buying a suit or dress, then wears it publically and gossips to anyone who will listen about how ugly their very own outfit is to their friends. Why would you purchase a relationship you don't like, make public appearances with the person, knowing the person belongs to you, having chosen that relationship before all your friends and family and have the nerve to publically criticize what you orchestrated?

I remember when Danielle and I were in the infancy stages of our dating courtship, we spent much time on the phone just talking and our phone conversations lasted for hours. Reflecting on how good our transparency was in our dating phase made me think about my immaturity in past dating relationships when I tried to play cool, refusing to effectively communicate my real feelings because the enemy tricked me into thinking that if I kept everything honest and displayed the REAL ME to people, no one would like the REAL ME in my ignorance. Therefore, when I matured as a child of God, I made up my mind that whoever God has for me, I was going to keep it real, with full disclosure about what I liked, disliked, my past and all that I was willing to accept and Danielle agreed to do the same. Each time we talked for hours, she got a chance to know the real Bryan C. Jones and I got to know the real Danielle. In the midst of being in an honest friendship and dating Danielle, I discovered how she embraced the real Christian man that she knew me to be without me having to feel like I had to protect myself or that I wasn't good enough if I was just plain me. God revealed to me that there is nothing that can stop the person whom He has for you from wanting to be with you, absolutely nothing! When God has someone for you, the things you think matter won't matter to your future spouse because they can see the inner beauty deep down within you. THAT PERSON can see the love that God has deposited into your heart clearly and I've learned for the right person to like you, you don't need to spray a whole bottle of Creed cologne on, always dress in fly a suit, or be the Sister with all the Mac makeup you own on your face to be loved, because God will give the person He has for your life the visibility to see the real you AND LIKE YOU!

In dating I strongly urge and recommend starting with a friendship devoid of any romantic or emotional connections, because you can really get to know someone without any attachments, titles, or pressures. Having a best a friend of the opposite sex gives you the opportunity to release yourself from the demands of impressing people, avoiding the pressures of feeling as though you have to be seen in such a high regard all the time. With that kind of friendship, you can communicate and share intimate details about your life, your feelings, the good, the bad, and the ugly. Marrying your best friend is one of the best ways to keep, develop, and continue a relationship of communication which ultimately gives you the best chance of working through your differences to stay together in a mutually beneficial, healthy, spiritual relationship.

Seasons of Relationship Growth

CHAPTER 7

Relationship Status: In a Relationship with Christ

*C*hange your spiritual relationship with God before you change your romantic relationship status with a potential mate for marriage. Before a person can be in a healthy dating relationship, they need to be in a healthy spiritual relationship with God, under the spiritual influence of the Lord.* Spiritual influence is what every marriage and potential dating relationship needs in order to operate. Before this happens, a person has to get into a relationship with Jesus Christ. The word of God is precise and clear on how a person gets into a right relationship with Jesus Christ. Frequently on FaceBook people exercise the right to inform their followers and friends of their relationship status on their personal profiles. The relationship status for some says "In a relationship" others may say "Single." The power of dating for those who are single can have many positives, but before you can enter into a relationship with anyone it is best to already be in an existing relationship with Christ. A relationship with Christ is the only relationship that has heavenly consequences, but it takes times to develop a daily relationship with Christ. While a person is single, they should take time to read God's Word, study the Word of God, and learn more about Jesus and His sacrifice for the sins of humanity. The strength of your personal relationship with Christ will lead you in making informed spiritual decisions on who you date and who you entertain marrying in the dating process. Dating can become an unpleasant process if you don't have a close, intimate, connective relationship with Christ. There are two types of relationship decisions one can make before deciding to marry someone. The first is a *spiritual decision* to marry someone, dating to find out if this person has sufficient enough spiritual character to consider as a potential mate for marriage. Let's not down play looks as they are very important, especially how people **LOOK** in the eyes of the Lord! *"The eyes of the Lord are in every place watching the good and the evil"* (Prov 15:3). For me physical attraction was very important, and I wasn't interested in marrying someone who I didn't find attractive. Physical attraction was important, but not enough, because in dating I learned someone could be fine and ugly all at the same time. My baby, my future wife wasn't just fine; she was and still is more beautiful on the inside than she is on the outside. Most importantly, one should decide to marry from a spiritual perspective, unfortunately, too many marriage relationships crumble, leaving a spouse hurt, broken, left with the burden to raise kids and struggling financially. The second relationship decision is an *unspiritual decision*. Many marriages never have a chance as one person or even both parties may have never intended to live the kind of Christian life that it takes for a marriage to survive. No marriage is perfect and yes, even Christian marriages are arduous and struggle to remain together as some Christian marriages fail too. However, my point is that one could be in a spiritually charged relationship where both participants are determined to be committed, living and operating within the marriage according to the principles, roles, and commandments God has given them to obey. *"Husbands, love your wives, just as Christ also loved the church and gave Himself up for her,"* (Ephesians 5:25). What makes a man refrain from cheating on his spouse? What can make a woman stop from being disrespectful to her husband? How would a child know

74

what a husband or wife should look like? It is through a person's love and obedience to God and the Word of God. A marriage devoid of the Word of God being practiced is a marriage that can easily be influenced with temptation and tainted with the desires of the flesh. (Heb 13:4). One who has not demonstrated the ability to commit to anything throughout their life may be very reluctant to commit to you; moreover, if they haven't committed themselves to the Lord, nothing binds them to commit to you in a marriage. I encourage everyone to get into a relationship with Jesus Christ so that you can become your Heavenly Father's child, receiving His Spirit which if you allow it, the Holy Spirit will guide you into controlling your behavior and decisions to align with God's will. God has to influence a person to develop and practice the kind of healthy behaviors that keep families together. Without knowing what healthy spiritual behaviors are, it would be very difficult to develop them out of thin air.

One time I asked a lady who was divorced, hurt and embarrassed because her ex-husband used to beat her, if she could go back in time and change one thing about her decision to marry her ex, what would that one thing be? In tears she said, "I was raised in church and believed in doing what the bible said and he wasn't, but I followed him anyway, but I never thought he could ever lay his hands on me." She said, "If I could, I would go back and find me someone who really lived by the Word of God." Though all relationships have challenges and even Christian men and women get into fights and make the same kind of mistakes sometimes as people in this world make, we should strive to find someone with a heart to love God, who doesn't want to let the Lord down, a person who at least answers to God, one who is willing to humble himself or herself to repent from mistakes, doing his or her best at avoiding behaviors that will be detrimental to the marriage and the family dynamic.

CHAPTER 8

Finders Looking for Keepers

In Proverbs 18:22 the writer says, *"He who finds a wife finds a good thing And obtains favor from the LORD."* This verse in Proverbs 18:22 doesn't describe the process of finding a wife as an easy thing, as the usage of the word **"finds"** is a verb which means **action** must taken by someone in the process of finding a wife. The original Hebrew word *"matsa"* that is translated into English as the word *"finds"* means **"to attain"** and is used 231 times in the bible and *"matsa"* is also translated as the word *"found"* as well. Proverbs 18:22 teaches us that the wife in the passage has to **be found,** which means, **before a woman can be found as a wife, she MUST possess the Godly attributes of a wife before she officially becomes a man's wife.** The motivation for spiritually driven women, who are desirous of being found, must be to possess the Godly attributes of a wife beforehand. Notice that Proverbs 18:22 says, *"he who finds a wife….,"* so the Godly wife should already have the skills, gifts, talents and traits of a wife, that are attractive to God and her future spouse even before marriage. The text doesn't say **He who finds a <u>Baby Mama</u> finds a good thing** or **He who finds a <u>Bae</u> finds a good thing;** neither does the text say **He who finds a <u>Side Chick</u> finds a good thing,** it says **He who finds a <u>Wife</u> finds a good thing.** (Prov 18:22)

If you are not a wife now, no worries, God is seeking to develop YOU into a wife right now, the same way He is desirous of developing some brother reading this book into a husband as well. The writer of Proverbs 18:22 makes a powerful declaration showing us the importance of being proactive, prepared, and ready to be found as someone who desires marriage, which should become motivation for someone to become what they need to, before they are found. Before a man finds a wife and before a wife is found, both parties need to be working to improve every aspect of their lives, spiritually, mentally, financially, and physically.

In His comparison to the Kingdom of Heaven, Jesus in Matthew 25:1-13 taught the parable of the ten virgins. Five virgins were wise, prepared to meet the Bridegroom, having their lamps filled with oil, but the five foolish virgins were unprepared, as a result, when the Bridegroom came back those foolish virgins weren't able to attend the wedding feast. (Matt 25:1-13) Have you ever been unprepared for something and lost out on a good opportunity? Being prepared to be found when someone comes to find YOU is a MUST. Be prepared. *It was paramount that women prepare themselves to be in a position to be useful for service to God, because if a woman has the spiritual characteristics of a wife, the Lord knows how to place her in a position to be noticed by a Godly man.* It's not by coincidence or happenstance that God can use the spiritual traits, qualities, and characteristics of a Godly woman for the service work in His Kingdom and bring a purpose driven spiritual man and woman together for marriage to be a blessing to His Kingdom. God placed Ruth in a position to be noticed by a spiritual and wealthy man named Boaz whom she ended up marrying (Ruth 2:1-7). God can bless YOU to be "found" if you have the kind of helpful qualities and characteristics that Ruth possessed. Ruth was *loyal, displayed kindness* (Ruth 2:11), *devoted herself to keeping the family together despite adversity* (Ruth 1:14), *willing to speak up for what she believed* (Ruth 1:16-17) *and not afraid to listen the counsel of an older woman* (Ruth 3:1-5). What makes the story of Ruth and Boaz even more interesting is the fact that **Ruth was the aggressor**. (Ruth 3:6-13) After meeting Boaz, Ruth was willing to put herself in a position to be noticed by Boaz through her service as a maid for him (Ruth 3:7-9) which allowed her to have favor with Boaz. Notice Boaz's response to Ruth after she placed herself in Boaz sight offering her service as a maid, which helped her to be noticed by him, *"Now, my daughter, do not fear. I will do for you whatever you ask, for all my people in the city know that you are a woman of excellence."* (Ruth 3:11) Before Ruth was chosen as a wife, she had already been raised to the status of being coined and called a **woman of excellence** by her future husband which means, God knows how to expose and direct, Godly, talented, skilled, and gifted women to the man God has destined for their lives when they posses Godly spiritual characteristics that He can use! (Ruth 3:11)

The Value of Choosing a Spiriutal Mate

What does God see in a husband or a wife before He positions a man to find a wife and a woman to be found as a wife? If you're reading this as a woman desirous of marriage, the question you must ask yourself is: Have I positioned myself spiritually to be found right now by a spiritual man or, for a man looking to find that right spiritual wife, are you the husband you need to be right now for a Godly wife? You certainly want to marry a spiritual person because marrying unspiritual people can lead to a lifetime of marital pain, and truthfully so could a spiritual person who refuses to live a Christ centered life. At least by marrying a committed spiritual person, you should be able to count on their consistent spiritual practice which should position your marriage to be blessed by God instead of having blocked blessings in an unspiritual marriage union devoid of practicing that which honors God. In choosing someone to operate in a spiritually driven marriage where both parties seek to please God, there are some indicators you must be aware of before choosing a spouse. I could not imagine being with someone I didn't feel comfortable praying with or someone who didn't pray at all. Having the weight and leadership responsibility of the marriage on the shoulders of a man who doesn't believe in God, live for Him, and refuses to pray to God for the safety and security of his family in faithful obedience, would be difficult to say the least. All the good things that women love and expect from men in terms of practicing monogamy, displaying Godly character traits described as fruits of the spirit (Gal 5:16-21) like love, kindness, gentleness, self-control, and rearing children in the Lord as a spiritual father, SHOULD NOT be expected (Eph 6:4) if a woman dates and marries an unspiritual man.

The Value of a Godly Spiritual Man

God was intentional and deliberate in preparing mankind for prominence in His biblical model for manhood. (Gen 2 & 3) The Lord God created Adam (Gen 2:7), then He planted a garden for the man Adam and placed him in the garden to cultivate and keep it (Gen 2:15). *"Then the LORD God took the man and put him into the garden of Eden to cultivate it and keep it."* (Gen 2:15). Sisters and brothers, ladies and gentleman, God is giving us a *model for manhood*! The man was *put* together by God (Gen 2:7), as a Father, God *positioned* man from the beginning to have everything he needed out of the ground such as trees for aesthetic beauty (Gen 2:9). The man Adam was given the resources he needed by God when the Lord *planted* a garden for him (Gen 2:8). The Lord put Adam in the garden giving him a job which gives a man a sense of *purpose*, then God instilled in Adam the task of *preservation* when He commanded the man to "keep it" referring to Adam's upkeep of the garden. (Gen 2:15). Then, God **provided** Adam with trees to eat in the garden for food (Gen 2:16) and lastly the Lord gave Adam a **partner**, to solve his need for social companionship (aloneness) by fashioning (building) a woman from one of the man Adam's ribs (Gen 2:22). God's blueprint, schematic, outline, and template for manhood is located in the Word of God as the Lord **put** man together, **positioned** man, **planted** for man, gave him a **purpose** by giving him a job, gave the ability to **preserve** resources, **provided food** and gave him a **partner**.

If a man has not humbled himself to be put together by God by being born again, lacks drive and purpose, failing to utilize the resources and skills God has given him, then those kinds of behaviors should cause the woman to stop and ask whether he possesses any Godly behaviors worthy for you to marry him. It never fails; I see spiritual women all the time who come to Church and presumably are committed to God, but choose men who do not work, stay home, have side hustles, but no main hustle, playing video games, smoking weed all day, getting high instead of getting by, and then the sister has the nerve to say she wants to marry him! When you marry someone that is living outside of their God given attributes you cannot expect their behavior to change because there is a chance that will never happen, and if you marry that person their future change would certainly be a miracle and not something you should expect. If that person never changes, a woman has to ask herself, is this the person I want to spend my life with? Is this the person I want to be the example for our children? If you are a Queen, is this person capable of being your King, if your spiritual purpose of dating is to find a Godly man? Frankly, how can you justify the decision to marry an ungodly man or how can a spiritual brother justify marrying an ungodly woman?

Make no mistake that the giftedness that exists within men is powerful when acted upon and utilized properly. Within the realm of manhood lies natural God given qualities which God has placed within men to be used, which helps us display the spiritual behaviors that should exist within a man before marriage. God placed Adam in the garden to cultivate it (Gen 2:15), showing us a map of Godly manhood that directs us to understand God's intent for man is to work by using his hands, his mind, possessing decision making capabilities, exercising the creative power and control to make intellectual decisions as Adam did by naming all the living creatures. (Gen 2:20)

Man Cave

A man cave is commonly coined as a place where men go to do what men do. Whether it's working, watching sports, enjoying good times with friends, exploring a hobby, sleeping or just having some alone time, that's what a man cave is for. I know what a man cave is and what men use them for, but I am going to use the term **"man cave"** in a slightly different way. Many times, people in our society participate in a **"man cave"** when we *"cave in"* on men, bashing and beating them up for their misfortunes, mistakes, and misconduct, instead of lifting them up. Rarely do men receive consistent positive praise when it's warranted, but in so many cases, men get a negative wrap for something. Not to ignore the fact that men mess up and need to be encouraged to live up to God's model for manhood, however, the truth is, many men and fathers didn't have fathers themselves or someone to teach them how to become a spiritual man. Men need positive spiritual friends, positive spiritual role models, and every man needs a father, a father figure or a spiritual mentor to help them. Men need someone to invest in them, work with them and show them the power of how God can help them reach their fullest potential. I don't want any admission of negative behavior on the part of men in this book to become an indictment on men, some spiritual death sentence or condemnation for being a bad man, as that is far from the case. Every man has struggles, destructive proclivities and personal problems that we all need to work on. The truth written in this book is intended for every reader to be clear, ***there is simply no guarantee that any unspiritual man or woman will ever change for the better, IF they do not practice and display existing spiritual behaviors in the dating process.***

The good news is, all hope is not lost, because some of the MOST *spiritual men* I know, used to be some of the most ***unspiritual men***, behaving just plain devilish, until they found their destiny, through a relationship with Jesus Christ. Before these men were **Super Saints**, they were **Super Sinners** and I know many preachers, church leaders and Christian men, who came to the Lord through a dating relationship with a Godly Christian woman. As a matter of fact, my own father came to the Lord because my mother was, and still is a Godly Christian woman, who led him to Jesus Christ when my parents were dating. After being invited to church to hear the gospel on a Wednesday night during bible class, my father came walking down the aisle to give his life to Jesus Christ and became a born again child of God! My mother's faith in God's purpose allowed my father to come to Jesus Christ, for which she and I are eternally grateful.

No man is perfect and every man needs some help, that's why the Word of God says, "Then the LORD God said, *"It is not good for the man to be alone; I will make him a helper suitable for him"* (Gen 2:18). If a woman's purpose is that of being a helper, many strong spiritual women have the spiritual influence and ability to lead their dating partners to Christ. (2 Peter 3:9) I want every brother reading this to know that you are wonderfully made and God didn't make a mistake when he made you. Your current or past behavior does not dictate what God can accomplish in your future! Remember, there were great men in the bible who made mistakes too, but God had a plan for their lives, just like He has a plan for your life. *Adam sinned, causing death to reign on the earth* (Gen 3:6-7), *Noah got drunk* (Gen 9:20-24), *Abraham lied* (Gen 20:2-3), *Jacob tricked his father, stealing his brothers blessing* (Gen 27), *Judah slept with his daughter in law and got her pregnant* (Gen 38:1-26), *Moses killed a man* (Ex 2:11-14), *David was an adulterous murderer* (2 Sam 12:9), *but a man after God's own heart, the wisest man,* **Solomon,** *foolishly, allowed his wives to turn his heart away from God* (1 Kings 11:1-4), *Peter used to curse and denied Jesus three times* (Matt 26:69-74*), Paul was formerly a blasphemer and a persecutor* (1 Tim 1:12-17), **but God still had a plan for all these great men of God**! There are some great men and women who have helped their dating partners, come to know Jesus Christ. Dating relationships can culminate in a fruitful *marriage with a wonderful spouse*, but sometimes dating relationships are orchestrated by God because someone needed a *marriage with Jesus Christ*. Sometimes when you're dating with a spiritual purpose in mind, God may ONLY be using you to help that person come into a relationship with Jesus Christ. *Remember, every soul is worth saving, but not every soul is worth marrying.*

Let's not all have a man cave and *"cave in"* on men, but *"aid in"* the personal development of men, lifting their spirits, encouraging them, praying for them and loving them. If you lead by the example of living a Christian life, you could help a man get closer to Christ, Who can teach them how to become a Godly man, husband and father, forever

Remember, every soul is worth saving, but not every soul is worth marrying.

being changed, all because you had a spiritual purpose to lead people to Christ.

Who's A Finder?

Finding a spouse requires someone interested in working to find things. Naturally, a man that is operating in his purpose knows who God has blessed and called him to be as a "finder," utilizing his strong work ethic, positioned by God as a worker. When I met my wife, Danielle, I was working. Working for whom? The Lord! I saw my wife for the first time at a church fellowship called the 5th Sunday Fellowship which her congregation was hosting in Liberty, SC. You may be thinking, okay, you met her at Church so what's the big deal? What makes how we met so powerful and such a big deal is what led to us meeting each other. Five years earlier, after having an encounter with God and having His purpose for my life revealed to me, I became a radical bible reader, memorized large portions of scripture and developed a personal ministry teaching students how to be saved according to the scriptures. I spent every moment I could, teaching the biblical plan of salvation to lost souls. I was doing one on one bible studies with five to ten people a week at times, sometimes baptizing up to three to four persons into Christ a week. Studying the bible became like breathing air for me, so I studied for hours, I very seldom watched TV; I was celibate for years. I traveled from Atlanta, GA to Anderson, SC four hours each Sunday to preach the gospel of Jesus Christ. My point in telling you this is that God positioned Danielle and me to meet and I believe he rewarded me for my dedication to Him with someone whom I could love. The Lord provided for me a helper suitable for me, based on the work I was doing for Him because I was working in His purpose to save lost souls. The biggest mystery and secret in Christianity is, if you work for God He will bless you, if you are working in His purpose and for His glory. God helped me find the person He had for my life not just because I was at a Church event; the Church event was the culmination of the process of God blessing me with what He believed I needed to continue to do His work and to take it to another level in my ministry. When a brother is in a ministry, working for God, as He did for Adam, the Lord will **put** you together, **position** you with what you need, **plant** a work for you, **place** you in the work, give you **purpose** and **preservation** in the work, **provide** for you and give you the **partner** you need in the work He desires for both of you.

A WIFE CAN BE FOUND by God for a man when she is operating in her natural God given purpose as a wife even before she is married, utilizing her gifts to fulfill what is lacking in the man as God created her to do. The wife (woman) was specifically created by the Creator (Gen 2:21-22) with a spiritual purpose in God's mind, being created *from* the man's rib (Gen2:22), created specifically *for* the man Adam and brought directly to the man by God (Gen 2:22). *"Then the LORD God said, "It is not good for the man to be alone; I will make him **a helper suitable for him**."* (Gen 2:18) Again in Genesis 2:20, God's Word says, *"The man gave names to all the cattle, and the birds of the sky, and to every beast of the field, but for Adam there was not found **a helper suitable for him**."* Notice that in Genesis 2:18 God said, *"**I will make him**,"* which should give every unmarried man who desires to be married hope, courage, and confidence to know not only does God recognize that being alone is problematic for man, He takes the initiative to make for you what He knows you need! God is a Maker, One who knows how to craft, a Creator and Designer of the person whom He ultimately has for your life, Tailor making her just for you! The problem with most dating relationships is that people don't use the same criteria that God uses to evaluate people when making decisions as to who a man ought to be with, therefore sometimes people choose a person that God would have never chosen for you. The question for those desirous of marriage is, based on your commitment to God, your ability to comprehend what God looks for when placing people into a spiritually compatible relationship and the spiritual qualities you should be seeking to desire, do you truly believe that God has made the person you're dating RIGHT NOW or THE PERSON you aspire to marry, specifically just for you? If not, you certainly have some decisions to make. In terms of the woman (wife) being found by a man, the specific purpose of God creating the woman (wife) was the fact that there was no one "*found*" that qualified as a "helper suitable for him" (Gen 2:18;20). In the dating process, a future wife should be at least three things: *1) A Communicative Vessel, Who Supplants Man's Loneliness 2) A Helper 3) A Helper that is Suitable for Him*

Suitability

A woman could be a helper, but not suitable in the eyes of God for every Godly man, just the Godly man whom God intended for her. It's glaringly apparent from the first human relationship that God was interested in certain criteria within the framework of the marriage dynamic, to exist and govern as a model for marriages. God looks at marriage as a spiritual institution with His commandments existing as the governing spiritual instructions for His people. Let's look at the suitability concept in a spiritual marriage.

A Communicative Vessel, Who Supplants Man's Loneliness

As I articulated in the aforementioned paragraph, a potential wife should be a **Communicative Vessel,** helping to obstruct man's loneliness. *Communication is the relationship oxygen the relationship and future marriage needs to breathe.* The man (Adam) that God created needed someone to solve the man's (Adam's) loneliness issue. The physical presence of having a compatible, reliable, and committed spouse is wonderful, but my suspicion is that most men are like "Akeem," Eddie Murphy's character in the movie, "Coming to America," when he said, *"I want a woman that's going to arouse my intellect as well my loins."* God Created the woman to satisfy that loneliness void in a man's life, so being physically absent fails in helping with that physical void and perhaps an intellectual void in the social dynamic of stimulating interest through conversation in a man's life, which should raise questions as to whether this woman meets the suitability of being that man's helper. If the man needs someone to talk to, he should be able to talk to his wife, but in the dating process, if a woman does not have the communicative skills in that area, then that should be a major red flag. Many people fail to communicate and shut down when problems arise because of their displeasure, hurt, or dissatisfaction with an outcome, problem, or issue. Without communication, a man or a woman will never know what the problem is, how to address it, solve it, listen and effectively help with dealing with the issue. Please understand that God would have never

Communication is the relationship oxygen the relationship and future marriage needs to breathe.

created a helper suitable for man if men didn't need some help! I want to get this out loud and clear, **MEN NEED HELP!** That's why God said *"I will make him a **helper** suitable for him* (Gen 2:18). I'm pretty sure that hundreds, no doubt thousands of women who read this will say AMEN to that, because it's true! However, if a woman never wants to communicate, that lack of communication defeats the very purpose, the very thing God created the woman for. (Gen 2:18; 20) It's certainly a two sided street with both men and women being responsible parties in effectively communicating, but for the sake of addressing the suitability issue I'm merely emphasizing the role of dating a woman who has consistently demonstrated the ability to communicate, before a spiritual man decides to marry her. If there is a lack of transparency and communication in the dating process it's possible, likely, and almost certain that the problem will implode in the marriage process. Most issues, discrepancies, quirks, and qualms could usually be solved by addressing the issue early on through the avenue of communication. However, if issues are not properly treated, something small, tiny, or myopic in the grand scheme of things could end up being colossal if it's not properly addressed, as small things fester in people just like nasty infections and before you know it the thing that started out small has manifested itself into something huge. Is the person you're dating an effective communicator? If so, if you're thinking about potentially marrying them and considering them as a mate for marriage, have you had a conversation where you have communicated about the things needed to make that kind of decision? I know plenty of people who have refused to receive pre-marital counseling because they actually have convinced themselves they have discussed it all, or they didn't want to know what they needed to know for fear that it would end the relationship. So, they get married and the very thing that ends the relationship is the thing pre-marital counseling was designed for them to disclose and discuss before getting married. A lack of willingness to effectively communicate should, would, and could be looked at as detrimental to the relationships future, as it is devoid of the co-existing social need of both the man and woman.

The second thing every woman needs to have in terms of suitability is the consistency of demonstrating herself as a helper. Is the woman you're dating a helper, healer, hurter, harmer, or hinderer? As I previously stated, we men need some help. Women are so powerful in demonstrating so many unique God given abilities that God has gifted them, which have effectively added incalculable value in many areas throughout man's anthropological existence. A helper is one who helps a person in a particular area where something is absent, lacking, devoid of substance or needs improvement, as a helper provides help. Adam (man) was blessed by the Creator to have a woman created specifically for him, brought to him with the Godly purpose of being God's answer to man's deficiencies. As I write this section of the book, I'm thanking God for blessing me with a wife who helps me every day. Just being there for me helps me, but my wife also works as an administrator at our Church. My wife mails visitor letters weekly, purchases supplies, proofreads my letters and devotions, meticulously keeps records, supports me, encourages me, takes care of our home, cleans the church building, decorates the church fellowship hall for events, encourages women, prays with me, thinks about the needs of members in the congregation, visits members in the hospital with me and when I can't, takes care of me, travels with me to support my preaching everywhere I go, gives helpful thoughts, has insightful ideas, listens to me, challenges me and charges me nothing as my stylist who tells me what kind of crazy colored socks I ought not wear when they do not match with anything I'm wearing. She is not perfect, but she is perfect for me, helpful, loving, insightful, and wise are all understatements for her. Her value to me literally defies description and articulation. God gave me, as He did so many other Godly men, what I needed for my social deficiencies and that was help, He gave me what I needed for my emotional deficiencies and that was help. Then, the Lord gave me what I needed to work for the Lord and that surely was some help! I'm bragging on God because He created for me what He knew I would need that I didn't even know I needed which was help. God gave me a wife who makes me better and I am grateful. If men have a God given vision in which they are operating in their God given purpose, they need help, not hurt, harm, or a hindrance. Too many men are in relationships with women who constantly seem like adversaries to their men. For some men, no matter what he does, it's never enough, it's never appreciated by their woman and instead of celebrating their man's accomplishments or achievements, I've heard some women say, "That's what you're supposed to do as the man." Satan has gotten a hold of too many good relationships and misconstrued the praise God should be receiving in the marital dynamic as a husband's success should be celebrated as the wife's success and vice versa. Why are men and women at war, seemingly against each other operating as adversaries and competitors as if they are on different teams instead of helping one another? The enemy has obstructed God's original intent of oneness. *"The man said, This is now bone of my bones, And flesh of my flesh; She shall be called Woman, Because she was taken out of Man." For this reason a man shall leave his father and his mother, and be joined to his wife; and they shall become one flesh"* (Gen 2:23-24). Although they are two separate individuals, the man and woman share an intimately connective relationship with each other to the degree they became one flesh together with God. If man and woman are one, why do they sometimes

If man and woman are one, why do they sometimes operate individually, separately, or against each other?

operate individually, separately, or against each other? That certainly was not God's design, so the question would be, who owns the copyrights to the marital design when the relationship is operating with a selfish *me first mentality?* My argument would certainly be in favor of the enemy as one who has crafted that design which makes relationships even more difficult than they already are to co-exist healthily therein. This world needs marriage relationships, showcasing Godly couples who have no desire to hurt, harm, or hinder each other, but to love one another more than themselves. I find it interesting that Adam was given the ability and creative freedom by God to name the animals, but didn't have a wife to give a name to (Gen 2:19-20) It's interesting that God never instructed the man Adam to name his wife, but instinctively he gave her a name that represented the connection God provided by taking her from the flesh of man. The name "woman" which Adam gave his wife, possesses the word "man" within the name "wo**man**," which was a name expressive of the connectivity man would enjoy with his wife whom God had joined him together with (Gen 2:23). A name is important as it signifies and symbolizes the physical bonding of a husband and wife together as well as the spiritual joining of man and woman in the covenant relationship bond of marriage.

A Helper Suitable for Him

Lastly, viewing God from the perspective of a Creator should cause one to view REVELATIONSHIP's, fruitful dating relationships and Godly marriages, in a different positive light. *"In the beginning God created the heavens and the earth."* (Genesis 1:1) God already existed before the beginning began with the Word. (John 1:1) No one forced God to create the heavens and the earth, and God never had to create mankind, but He did because He is a Creator, He's Creative. God created the universe and all that is within it including mankind. (Gen 1 & 2) I want you to envision the creative design of our Creator, notice the trees, sky, plant life, vegetation, oceans, mountains, the sun, moon, stars, rainbows, land animals, and even yourself! The human body itself is an amazing creation of interlocking systems all functioning together for human beings to have life, health and blood running through our veins. What an Amazing God! You are a design of the Creator no matter how you got here, no matter what the circumstances were which led to getting you here. You are a special design. God owns the copyrights to your design as He used His intellectual property to create you. If you truly believe God is the Architect and Creator of the world, Who as a matter of fact, Is the very first Interior and Exterior Designer, you can be confident in His ability to create someone specifically for you! The Creator can create someone for you just like He did for the man, Adam. Here's one thing I'm certain of, that God sees your vision and knows what you need. It is fully realistic that God has already created the person for you, a helper suitable for you, as He did with Adam and is waiting on you to get into His purpose so that He can unfold your blessing to you. (Gen 2:18; 20)

"So God created man in his own image, in the image of God created he him; male and female created he them." (Gen 1:27) If God created you and me in His image, which He certainly has, that means if we are not being creative as the God in whose image we were created, then we are not exercising all of our rights and privileges and living beneath our spiritual and creative means. I am telling you this because you can use the power of creativity in your life and it's possible that God can bless you to be found or find the helper suitable for you through your creativity. You are creative, different, and talented in your own right, but many times we operate outside of our natural creativeness and fail to externally use

what God has given us internally in terms of creativeness. God created us in His own image and created the heavens and the earth for us. It would be reasonable for God to ask us what we have created for Him. What ministries, businesses, spiritual endeavors, and opportunities to share your verbal testimony, good works, and good deeds have you created for the purpose of using your God given creativity to glorify God? The very creativity you use to glorify God could be the very creative process by which God uses to allow you to meet the mate for marriage He has created for you! I believe that many of us frequently allow the enemy to coerce, construe, constrain, conflict, and condition our minds to commit the catastrophic sin of allowing failure to become our fear, thus blocking the focus of our God given ability to be the creative people we are created to be. Even if we simply allow the Word of God to transform our lives, transform our behavior and transform our labor, then God has created a new person in us through Jesus Christ. *"Therefore if any man be in Christ, he is a **new creature**: old things are passed away; behold, all things are become new."* (2 Corinthians 5:17)

The need for a suitable helper is essential for a man, but the notion has repercussions for men and women. Some men would never need a suitable helper if they are not doing anything worthy of needing help. Working for God in a ministry that brings humanity closer to Jesus is the best job in the world, even more significant than the President of the United States of America. God can bless two co-existing workers of the Kingdom of God to be drawn to each other like two magnets on to metal from opposite sides of the world. The icing on top of the marriage cake is that God describes a Godly man, finding a Godly wife as a *"good"* thing. (Proverbs 18:22) A Godly, graceful, gentle, grounded, good hearted, giving, God fearing wife is a good thing. It's interesting that the Proverb writer didn't say that marriage was a good thing, although marriage truly is a good thing, because God created it and all that God created is good. (Gen 1:31) Why would God's Word descriptively use the adjective "good" to describe a wife being a good thing? There are unlimited possibilities of what a man and woman can do for God to glorify Him when two people with complimentary social and spiritual characteristics are joined together to create something historic, something great, something awesome, and that greatness can take place when there is a great woman to aid and help the man. Long before Barack and Michelle Obama, Prince Harry and Meghan Markle, or Jay - Z and Beyonce, there were biblical power couples like Adam and Eve, Abraham and Sara, Isaac and Rebekah, Jacob and Rachel, Ruth and Boaz, David and Abigail, Elkanah and Hannah, Xerxes and Esther, Priscilla and Aquila, and Joseph and Mary the mother of Jesus Christ. All of these couples were divinely aligned by God and each served their own specific purposes in glorifying God. In my finite wisdom, I've learned that God knows who completes the man and who completes the woman. If God was ready to bless you with your dream spouse, what would you do specifically for God for the rest of your life that would aid in God's purpose to redeem mankind back to Himself through His Son Jesus Christ? Your answer to that question may determine the direction you can take to honor God, and along the way He will give you what you need to accomplish His will. You don't have to be a Preacher or a Preacher's wife to work in God's purpose, just a grateful dedicated laborer who believes in using your gifts to advance God's Kingdom agenda tirelessly.

Cold Fridays And Lonely Saturdays

Dating was tough for me because I was so picky. It's really not a sin to be picky, the positive part of being picky is that you narrow your search criteria, but consequently you have to widen your search parameters to meet people. In my case, my spirit was settled because I trusted God that I would find someone for my life that I could fall deeply for and love, but I was very deep into the nuts and bolts of ministry which occupied all my time. I made up my mind that I wouldn't settle for less than I had prayed for. Consequently, I had a lot of cold Fridays and lonely Saturdays. My friends still included me on group text messaging and all my friends were out and about having a good time and here I am on the couch bound by God to do things right as an example. By the time I had met Danielle I had been celibate for years. I'm not telling you this because I'm looking for any kudos because God expects His people to be pure until marriage and I had previously broken my purity through fornication in the past so I repented of premarital sex and later entered into ministry as my calling was and is to preach and teach God's Word. I wanted to be a major player in the Church, not the player of the Church. I always knew and believed that I had to have that *"it"* factor, when you know **"it"** you feel **"it"** and God confirms when the person has *"it"*! That's what I needed. Being a young Preacher always trying to be an example of living right wasn't hard, what I was most concerned with was finding the right person for my life who God wanted me to be with, so that I could do all I desired for Him. Danielle and I had been dating for a few months and by that time I knew she was the one for me. Now, I consider myself not necessarily a Mama's boy as one who has a controlling Mother who makes decisions for him, I'm just a Mama's boy who is extremely close to his Mother who simply values her Godly spiritual wisdom. My mother means a lot to me and so did her approval of my dream wife. My mother is spiritual, very spiritual with knowledge, wisdom and insight from the word of God that is deep, really deep, but she gave me some simple advice. She told me to pray that God would show me the face of the person He wanted me to marry, so I did. I prayed, I didn't know or even think about how God would do this, but I tucked that prayer away in the back in my mind and didn't think about it anymore. Months later I woke up one morning on the couch of my apartment around 6:00am, reached on the floor for my phone and the first thing I saw was a picture of Danielle! She was smiling as beautiful as she could be and it dawned on me that this is the face that I had prayed about months before that God was showing me! If you could have seen me, I was jumping up and down in my apartment (probably waking up my neighbors), as if I had just won a championship! This is one of the many confirmations God gave me which revealed who He wanted me to be with to conduct Kingdom business with, as bone of my bone and flesh of my flesh (Gen 2:23).

STUDY GUIDE

1.) Find out the needs of people and develop a deep desire to help people by solving their needs. Men always need help. God will position you to be noticed by the right man when being a helper becomes who you are for humanity, not just something you do to find a man.

2.) Work on your communication skills. The only way to get better communicating is to communicate more.

3.) Work for God. Find an attractive ministry which highlights your skill set. Spend time working to refine and improve in that ministry each day.

4.) Assess your suitability for a mate for marriage and your work ethic to advance the Kingdom. If either one of those isn't up to par, change it today for the better. The only person that can change your suitability for becoming someone's spouse is you. Change may be difficult for some, but it's necessary for success.

5.) Improve being a better you each day. No one is going to be happy with you, if you're not happy with yourself.

6.) Love people by helping them. Help an older person walk into the doors of a business and you could meet someone in that business that you may end up walking down the aisle with to marry next year. Never underestimate the power of demonstrating love to humanity, God will bless you.

7.) Trust God to lead you to your "good thing" or become the "good thing" that God draws a Godly man to.

CHAPTER 9

Finding Your Dream Spouse

The best way that I can describe marrying Danielle is that it's like being blessed by God beyond my most imaginative dreams, waking up from a dream where I found my dream spouse and realizing it was true and hitting the lottery all at the same time (even though I don't gamble or play the lottery). It reminds me of the Ruth and Boaz narrative when Ruth went through so much in her life dealing with trials, up's and down's, but trusted Naomi's advice which allowed her to ultimately marry Boaz (Ruth 2:22-23). Ruth possessed a relentless, obedient, determined spirit and because of her dedication to family and loyalty, God saw something in her that He could use so the Lord placed Ruth in a position to be noticed by Boaz. The beauty of Ruth and Boaz's marriage was the fact that God divinely orchestrated the relationship, so that their marriage would culminate in producing a son named Obed, who was in the Davidic family lineage that the Messiah, Jesus Christ, came from (Ruth 4:16-21). God had a plan for Ruth, Boaz, and Naomi. God soothed the brokenness of Ruth and the Lord gave Naomi a grandchild to love even after all the tragedy she faced and finally Boaz received the wife he needed as he sought to keep God's commandments.

My point in telling you this is that if you are faithful, the Lord knows how to bless His people, and if you do what's right while you are single, God knows how to place you in a position to be noticed by the man or woman who needs to notice you. Sometimes you can meet someone, but never notice them. However, when God has that special person for your life, He will make it clear by positioning and orchestrating the relationship where your paths cross and you notice each other. Before I got married, I used to hear people say all the time, when you find the right one, you will know it. I found that to be true, but in a spiritual way. It was not about whether I wanted to marry Danielle, the question for me was, does God want me to marry Danielle, and the question for her was does God want me to marry Bryan? So many times people enter into marriages and relationships for the sole purpose of physical enjoyment and to quench the loneliness, and I certainly understand that. However, God always has a bigger purpose for marriage. Can these two people come together taking what they both bring to the table and collectively and spiritually make a larger contribution to God and the work in the Kingdom of God?

Finding your dream spouse is not about finding a perfect person as only One Perfect Person exists, which is the Messiah Himself, Jesus Christ. Years before I was married, I would always envision that my dream spouse would be someone I was attracted to, someone who would be my best friend, and a person who I could trust with my life. Most importantly, my dream spouse was always one who was a consistent, practicing Christian in the body of Christ, who is committed to keeping faith in Christ until the Lord comes back or death. That's what was attractive for me, a non-skeptical, faithful, believing woman.

My Good Thing

Ever since I was a young boy I have dreamed of marrying someone that was truly a fit for me. Someone who gets me and I get her. I dreamed of having someone who laughs at my jokes or sarcasm even when I'm not that funny. I desired someone that I could be silly and corny with; someone who would even find that attractive, in a weird kind of way, because she understands me. I needed someone who could see the best in me, even when I was displaying the worst in me. I too, like most men, needed to be physically attracted to my spouse. On the outside my wife Danielle is beautiful, really beautiful and physically intimidating to a lot of people because it is truly rare that you can find someone so stunningly beautiful, but humble, never taking herself too serious. However, Danielle is TRULY more beautiful on the inside than she will ever be on the outside and that truism speaks volumes of her spiritual character and the God she serves. Danielle has a genuine loving spirit within her that only God could give. God gave her the personality and spirit to see the positive side of things first before dwelling on the negative. She is a woman who will tell you that she has been through some things and is far from perfect, but always trusts God to help her find her way. Danielle is so caring, loving, sweet, thoughtful, and genuinely kind. She would go out of her way to help anybody including strangers because of her love for God's people. I'm telling you this to show you what God can do for you when He blesses you to find your "Good Thing." Physical attraction has always been important to me, but it wasn't and has never been enough to sustain me. God blessed my wife Danielle to encompass all of the physical attributes that attracted me, but the spiritual attributes that God blessed her with are what hooked me. What should make a person really attractive is their spiritual attributes because those are the attributes that have eternal value, unlike physical attributes, which fade away over time.

Age Ain't Nothing But A Number

I've learned that we may think we know exactly what we need in a mate for marriage, but unfortunately the enemy knows how he can mess you up, blinding your vision to the person God has placed in your life, if you're more concerned with placing a check mark on your list of requirements of the person you desire, instead of the person that God has for you. God knows how to give you a "Good Thing" and if you remove an "o" from the word "Good," then your "Good thing" becomes a "God Thing." A "God Thing" may only appear once in your life and it may not appear to have every detail on your list that you listed beforehand. However, in actuality you may gain much more than what you ever wanted or even imagined, you just didn't know it because you bought into preconceived expectations of your own "Good Thing" when God supplied you with a "God Thing!" God has a sense of humor, because He knows how to make something appealing to you that you may have thought you would never find appealing. I almost missed out on having the love of my life because of one of those details which was the age factor.

My wife is older than me. This should not have been an issue, but I brought my preconceived expectations to the dating relationship and the age difference was not something that I ever wanted to waiver on in the past. But when I met Danielle and got to know her, the Lord quickly showed me that there was so much value in a woman who was older than me. I learned that my baby was wise, smart, settled, calm, traveled, experienced, real, and passionately driven about God in a way that was undeniably attractive to me. One has to make a decision when you have a detailed list of must have's and deal breakers because God knows how to call an audible and change the play in your dating relationships.

In the game of American football, the Quarterback is the most important player on the field, he is the leader and makes sure everyone on the team knows what the play is so that the team can successfully execute the play in hopes of getting his team to the end zone to score. However, before any play is executed, sometimes the Quarterback looks at how the defense is lined up and sees something he can exploit to effectively march his team down the field to score, so he then calls an audible. An audible happens when the Quarterback gives a verbal command to change the play before the original play happens, because he has seen something he feels that would work better for the team to score. It's interesting that when the Quarterback calls an audible and changes the play his teammates do not quit, walk off the field or give up; they have so much trust and faith in the Quarterback's vision and decision-making capability to see something that they can't see, they go along with the new play and execute it as they trust in the Quarterback to get them to the end zone through a different route. God is the Quarterback in every dating relationship, especially when He calls an audible during a break up or He gives you something or someone you did not expect Him to. If God has positioned you to get to know a spiritual person, a loving person, a person of integrity, knowledge, character, commitment, and dedication to Him, you may need to trust that God has seen something in a person that will make your relationship successful that you cannot see or could not see, because as your Quarterback, He knows how to call a spiritual audible and change the play. As a Good Quarterback, God wants to take your purpose driven dating relationships, assemble a spiritual team with you and your spouse, and march your marriage down the field of life, so that you can score a Heavenly touchdown in the end zone and make it to heaven together spending eternity with God!

God opened my eyes to see that *age isn't anything but a number,* and the Almighty God should not be limited to the calculatory limitations of our human finite minds. God had potentially blessed

God should not be limited to the calculatory limitations of our human finite minds.

102

me with my dream wife and I was convinced that I was not about to overlook someone I knew that God created for me, so the predetermined age thing I had before I met Danielle quickly became a non-issue for me because of my faith in the God Who divinely gave me a wife, my "Good Thing."

Hannah's Prayer

The real reason I thought I needed someone younger when I met Danielle was the fact that I always wanted children. For years, I have envisioned having a little man, a mini me or a little girl to raise and you know I've had big spiritual plans for my future child or children. However, in dating, I bought into the idea of what most doctors suggest in terms of having children in younger years which would increase the chances of pregnancy as many doctors will tell you that the likelihood of getting pregnant over the age of thirty-five is possible but high risk because of the woman's age, and it may not happen. But I read somewhere that Sarah, Abraham's wife had a baby at 90 years old, so I know that all things are possible for those who believe! (Gen 17:1-22; Mark 9:23)

BEFORE we got married, Danielle and I discussed what it would be like if we didn't have children of our own. How would we feel? Would there be a void? It was important to discuss the possibility of not having children if the Lord chose not to open her womb because I did not want my wife to feel any less than a woman or feel that she owed me anything or that I would love her any less if we didn't have children. Through faith, God helped both Danielle and me overcome those concerns even though we both needed to be aware of the challenges that come with pregnancy over the age of thirty-five. We decided that we would be happy with each other and our marriage relationship would be complete with or without children even though we both desperately wanted kids. Making that decision eliminated the pressure of having children and we put all the pressure on God to do it for us, but if He decided not to, we would be satisfied with each other and explore other options in the future.

Danielle and I got married on June 14, 2014, and it was the best day of my life with the exception of the day I got baptized into Christ on September 3, 1997. The day we got married, I remembered echoing the sentiments of Solomon when he said, *"You are altogether beautiful, my darling, And there is no blemish in you."* (Song of Songs 4:7) A few weeks after we got married, an older man asked me did we have any kids yet and I told him no and he said, "don't worry, practice makes perfect," so we practiced, practiced, and practiced some more! We would always pray that God would bless us to have a child. We both always wanted a child of our own to raise, helping them to contribute to the world, to the Kingdom of God and to bless our parents to be grandparents. Danielle's Mother and Father had three children, but no grandchildren of their own. My Mother has me, as her only child, but no grandchildren. So for our parents it would be beyond exciting for God to bring a grandchild to both sides of our families. We prayed and prayed some more, continuing to believe God would bless us with a child. ***We prayed Hannah's prayer.*** In 1 Samuel 1 there was a woman by the name of Hannah who was married to a man named Elkanah (1 Samuel 1:2). The problem was, Hannah had no children and was barren. The word of God says, "….the LORD had closed her womb" (1

We prayed Hannah's prayer.

Samuel 1:6). This passage in 1 Samuel 1:5-6 is very interesting to me because it suggests that God had a purpose for closing Hannah's womb. It could be that God sometimes has to allow things to be closed, until He can get His people to a place where we trust in Him to give us what we need so that he can get His glory when He opens things. Because of her condition Hannah was desperate, destitute, defeated, distressed, depressed, and mentally debilitated, not being able to give her husband whom she loved a son, so Hannah prayed making a vow to God. *"She, greatly distressed, prayed to the LORD and wept bitterly. She made a vow and said, "O LORD of hosts, if You will indeed look on the affliction of Your maidservant and remember me, and not forget Your maidservant, but will give Your maidservant a son, then I will give him to the LORD all the days of his life, and a razor shall never come on his head."* (1 Samuel 1:10-11) If God gave Hannah a son, she vowed to give the son back to God for the service work of the Lord. *"It came about in due time, after Hannah had conceived, that she gave birth to a son; and she named him Samuel, {saying}, "Because I have asked him of the LORD."* (1 Samuel 1:20) After looking deeply at this wonderful story of prayer, faith, and perseverance it is not surprising or shocking that God would give Hannah a son and allow her to give him back to God. Seeing Hannah's courage to give up her only son, God knew that He would one day give His only begotten Son Jesus Christ, for the service and salvation of mankind (Isaiah 9:6; Mark 10:45).

On February 24, 2016, Danielle and I went to the Doctor and confirmed that she was pregnant! God is so good! We were so excited that God had blessed us and answered our prayers. We vowed to give our child back to God as we prayed Hannah's prayer. I told Danielle if we have a girl we would train her to become a Preacher's wife and if we had a boy I would teach him to follow in his father's footsteps and become a Preacher. I'm not sure how keen Danielle was on the idea, but because she was so happy she just went along with me and smiled. We planned out how we were going to let our parents know that Danielle was pregnant so we drove to see my Mother to tell her in person and later on we took Danielle's mom out to dinner to tell her. Both of our Mothers were shocked and didn't even believe it at first until we convinced them with pictures of the ultra sound! They were completely overcome with joy. Danielle quickly made some adjustments in her diet and kept all of her Doctor's appointments as we wanted to have a healthy pregnancy welcoming our first child into the world. I remember how we started a list of boys and girls names narrowing down the list each day to the names we would choose.

We decided that we would announce our pregnancy news to our Church family once Danielle got out of the first trimester. I planned out how I was going to present our pregnancy to the Church and what I was going to say. Days before that Sunday, we planned to announce one of our happiest moments in our marriage thus far, we had another Doctor's appointment on Wednesday March 30th 2016. Every other appointment went well except for this one. The Doctor discovered on a routine ultrasound that there was no longer a heartbeat and our child was gone just that quick. As the Doctor advised us of the findings, the Lord gave my Wife a peace. I thanked God because this was not a normal peace; it was the peace that Paul talked about in Philippians 4:6-7, the peace that surpasses all understanding. Immediately tears came down my eyes without thinking, but Danielle showed much resilience, after hearing the news her facial expression was not one of defeat, but one of accomplishment. It was as if Danielle simply appreciated God for allowing us to get that far because the Lord allowed us to defy the odds, a view I to soon shared where we showed appreciation for God in the joy we found in that pregnancy, as we experienced something that some people have never gotten a chance to experience. God gave me a sermon to preach to encourage myself and my wife in the car after we just received the bad news. The sermon God gave me was a revelation about pain. I told Danielle that the pain we are experiencing right now with the loss of our child could be because God was saving us from some future pain. The bright side was that God blessed us with a child that was now with the Lord, who we will meet one day in heaven. We believed in that sermon and prayed together in the car and never looked back. I do wish that if it was God's will our child could have been spared, but it obviously wasn't His will. I am just so thankful that God blessed us to get through that together and grateful for our spiritual walk with the Lord that got us through. I couldn't imagine going through that without someone with the kind of spirit like my Wife has. God thank you for bringing us through that storm, wounded, but not weary, giving us hope in the resurrection to be reunited with our child one of these days. Thank you Hannah for inspiring us to pray and vow to God, you are one of the reasons we got that far. Danielle and I firmly believe that we have a child living in glory and that God is able to bless us with another child. We are still praying. Stay tuned…

CHAPTER 10

The Blessing of Being His Good Thing

A Testimony by Danielle Jones

Relationship! Wikipedia's definition of relationship is "a strong, deep, or close association between two or more people." It is an essential role to the overall human experience. Whether it's between a parent and child, a husband and wife, family and friends, or mankind and its Creator, almost from the very moment we come into the world we instinctively desire to have a relationship. My experience has been no different! From a young girl developing friends and family relationships, to a young woman desiring that next level of relationship, marriage and children, I had to first discover the most important relationship that would ensure my success. That is my relationship with our Lord and Savior, Jesus Christ. It has not always been an easy journey, but nothing worthwhile comes easily. Just look at what Jesus endured!

Like many others, my relationship journey had been hindered by mistakes, wasted time, compromises, and just a simple lack of knowledge on how to be a "good thing" and how to attract the type of man, God desired for me and not just what I wanted for myself. When I finally had enough of failing on my own, I said, "Okay, Lord! I'm ready to do it your way!" I completely changed my m. o. (modus operandi or mode of operation) to God's m. o. I let go of all of my worldly acquaintances and temptations and decided to focus on being thankful for the life God has given me and how I can use it to glorify Him. We had a motto at my previous church congregation that said, "Serving God by Serving Others." It inspired me to focus on God in every aspect of my life.

Once you realize that God knows you better than you know yourself, He sees everything you do and you begin to truly care what He thinks about you, it is not hard to want to please Him. After all, God wants the best for you and He is the one who has nothing but the best to give you! Instead of focusing on relationships and things of this world, I just began to live my life desiring God's approval, looking for His guidance and being thankful for His many blessings. I spent time deepening my relationship with Him, knowing He is the only one who can give me the desires of my heart. We walked and talked together daily as we still do. Let me tell you, there is nothing more assuring than knowing that God has got your back! "Great is his faithfulness! Morning by morning new mercies I see!" (Lam 3:23 KJV) There is a peace in knowing that "all things work together for good to them that love God, and to them who are called according to his purpose." (Rom 8:28 KJV)

When I began to live in God's purpose for my life, amazing things began to happen. I finally had peace, joy, and love just living for and serving God. That is, the first and most important relationship that we must desire to have before marriage, because He must be the center of that marriage relationship for it to be successful and approved unto Him. Now, I had no idea how God would bring my prayers for a husband to fruition. I was just happy that He was in control and not me! That

I was just happy that He was in control and not me.

is what is so great about God! If you are living for Him and doing His will He will bless you beyond belief! Little did I know, one beautiful spring day while having a wonderful time serving at a church fellowship, I would get my first introduction to Minister, Bryan C. Jones, the man who God sent to find me and who would later become my husband.

From that first moment until two years later when God joined us together, you could see God's hand working it out and giving us confirmation that it was all in His plan. Since then, we have made each day a living testimony as to what God can do when you put Him first in your life. So, to all of you out there who desire that marriage relationship, don't forget that God first wants to have a relationship with YOU!

CONCLUSION

The best decision both my wife and I ever made was to dedicate our lives to God and to work in His Kingdom. You have gifts, talents, skills, and a vast array of creative abilities that the Lord desires to use. Position yourself to become a worker for the Lord, a dedicated laborer in the Church and all the things you desire will quickly have the ability to come to fruition as God knows your heart. If having a successful spiritually focused marriage was easy everyone could do it and figure it out, but it's not. Trust God to send you what you need, as long as God can see you doing something to advance His kingdom agenda consistently.

Don't worry about prospects, where you live, the size of your town or congregation you attend, as God doesn't need any of the things you think to bless you with someone He crafted for you. Don't spend your life miserably with someone who doesn't want to go to heaven or to live the way God desires. Get into God's purpose. Do things God's way, put the Lord first in your decisions, trust Him to guide you to who He wants for your life. Let God figure it out and keep having faith as you work for Him. You cannot go wrong with sacrificing your time, energy, money, effort, and life to work for the Lord. Any lost soul who God positions

Let God figure it out and keep having faith as you work for Him.

you to encourage and to form a relationship with Jesus Christ, could be the very person He places into your life as a lifelong friend, confidant, or even a spouse. Then, all of the tears you've shed, hurt and pain you have experienced in this life would then provide a powerful testimony that will give God glory, a testimony that God has given my wife and me. Jesus said, "The harvest is plentiful, but the laborers are few..." (Matt 9:37) Remember, if God's purpose becomes your purpose, He knows who loves Him and the Lord knows how to work out all things (good and bad) together for good, through His people. *"And we know that God causes all things to work together for good to those who love God, to those who are called according to His purpose."* (Romans 8:28) No marriage is perfect, mine included, but working for the Lord has been the most rewarding thing in my life and that is how God gave me, "My Good Thing." God can do the same for you! Let's get to work!

BECOMING A CHRISTIAN

Becoming a Christian requires *hearing* that Jesus Christ died, He was buried and He rose again from the dead on the third day, as a sin Sacrifice for the atonement of your sins according to the scriptures. (1 Cor 15:1-4)

Becoming a Christian requires *believing* that Jesus Christ died, He was buried and He rose again from the dead on the third day, as a sin Sacrifice for the atonement of your sins according to the scriptures. (Mark 16:15-16; 1 Cor 15:1-4)

Becoming a Christian requires a believer to *repent* (a change of mind), resulting from Godly sorrow incurred from past disobedience. (2 Cor 7:9-10)

Becoming a Christian requires a believer to *confess* Jesus Christ is both, Lord and Christ, the Son of God. (Acts 2:37; 8:37)

Becoming a Christian requires a believer to be *baptized into Christ* for the remission of sins. (Acts 2:38)

Remaining a faithful Christian *requires a lifetime commitment to the work of the Lord in His Church, practicing Christianity until death.* (2 Pet 1:5-11; 1 Thes 4:14-18; Rev 2:10)

**If you have any salvific questions and would like to request more information concerning biblical salvation, contact Bryan C. Jones Ministries at www.bryancjones.com by filling out the Contact Request section or email the *"Finding My Good Thing"* team at findingmygoodthing@gmail.com.

ABOUT THE AUTHOR

Bryan C. Jones was born in Greenwood, SC in 1979 to faithful Christian parents. He is the Evangelist and Minister of the Graceview Church of Christ, a rapidly growing, vibrant congregation of New Testament Christians in Anderson, SC. In January of 2015, Bryan led the Graceview congregation to start a Television broadcast called *"Passion for Christ"* which they use to spread the gospel of Jesus Christ to 1.4 million homes in Upstate SC, Northeast Georgia and Western North Carolina. Bryan also hosts a weekly Internet Radio program also called *"Passion for Christ"* which blesses many people throughout the country each week. He has preached numerous Gospel Meetings and Revivals in various states baptizing many souls into Christ. He has conducted many seminars, workshops and facilitates the **"Finding My Good Thing Singles Empowerment Seminar"** empowering single Christians through the wisdom in his book, *"Finding My Good Thing."* Bryan is a passionate student of scripture and a dynamic speaker whose love for the Lord is clearly articulated through his moving sermons from the Word of God. He will graduate in the Spring of 2019 with a Masters degree in Biblical Studies at Faulkner University. Bryan is married to Mrs. Danielle P. Jones, and they released a book in the Summer of 2018 that is available now titled, **"Finding My Good Thing,"** *How God Can Lead You To Your Future Spouse By Dating With A Spiritual Purpose.*

SPECIAL THANKS

Throughout my life God has blessed me to be surrounded with some wonderful family members, loved ones, and friends who have truly impacted my life tremendously; I want to recognize them for their incalculable deposit of love for me. My love, Danielle Jones, my Mother, Jo Ann Jones, my Father, Rufus L. Jones (RIP), Nancy Jones & the Jones family, Mary Crawford Orba (RIP) & the Crawford family, Bennie Crawford Sr., Lillie Crawford (RIP), Frances Jean Crawford, Willie Crawford, Bennie Crawford Jr., Lois Johnson, Robert Johnson, Xavier Armfield, Eric Martin, Byron White, Sylvia Anderson, John Marshall, I.V. White, Hosie Byrd Jr., Richard Barr, Ronald Wearing, Cornelius Edwards, Bryant Malone, Tacara Farmer, Mike Sayeh, Jim Clingman and also every member of the Graceview Church of Christ family who has encouraged, supported, and worked with me in my ministry throughout the years.

Thank you. – Bryan C. Jones

FOR MORE INFORMATION OR FOR BOOKING

Bryan C. Jones

PO Box 722

Anderson, SC 29622

678-382-7463

www.bryancjones.com
bryancjones79@gmail.com

findingmygoodthing@gmail.com

Made in the USA
Coppell, TX
05 December 2021

67260873R10076